MW00830754

Watch out for false prophets. They come to you in sheep's clothing, but inwardly they are ferocious wolves.

—Matthew 7:15 (niv)

MYSTERIES OF COBBLE HILL FARM

MYSTERIES OF COBBLE HILL FARM

Wolves in Sheep's Clothing

SANDRA ORCHARD

A Gift from Guideposts

Thank you for your purchase! We want to express our gratitude for your support with a special gift just for you.

Dive into **Spirit Lifters**, a complimentary e-book that will fortify your faith, offering solace during challenging moments. Its 31 carefully selected scripture verses will soothe and uplift your soul.

Please use the QR code or go to **guideposts.org/spiritlifters** to download.

Mysteries of Cobble Hill Farm is a trademark of Guideposts.

Published by Guideposts
100 Reserve Road, Suite E200, Danbury, CT 06810
Guideposts.org

Scripture references are from the following sources: *The Holy Bible, King James Version* (KJV). *The Holy Bible, New International Version* (NIV). Copyright © 1973, 1978, 1984, 2011 by Biblica, Inc. Used by permission of Zondervan. All rights reserved worldwide. www.zondervan.com.

Cover and interior design by Müllerhaus
Cover illustration by Bob Kayganich at Illustration Online LLC.
Typeset by Aptara, Inc.

ISBN 978-1-961441-11-8 (hardcover)
ISBN 978-1-961441-12-5 (softcover)
ISBN 978-1-961441-13-2 (epub)

Printed and bound in the United States of America
10 9 8 7 6 5 4 3 2 1

MYSTERIES OF COBBLE HILL FARM

Wolves in Sheep's Clothing

GLOSSARY OF UK TERMS

aye up • form of greeting in Yorkshire

bloke • man

boot • trunk of a vehicle

cheers • good wishes expressed at the start and/or end of a visit; an expression of gratitude

chuffed • pleased, delighted

daft • silly, foolish

dodgy • shady

gimmer • a female sheep in her second year who hasn't yet had her first lamb

grass on • report to the authorities

half-term break • a week-long break in the middle of a school term

having you on • duping or deluding you

knocking about • wandering

mate • friend

nick • steal

nob • a wealthy person, or someone of high position

pud • short for "pudding" in reference to any dessert course, not strictly the American pudding variety

tup • a ram

wellies • Wellington boots

CHAPTER ONE

"M y Yorkshire puddings always deflate," Harriet Bailey lamented to her patient neighbor, Doreen Danby, in Doreen's large farmhouse kitchen early Sunday evening. In the months since Harriet arrived from the US to take over her grandfather's veterinary practice, Doreen had helped her navigate traditional UK cuisine and so much more. Today they planned to tackle the temperamental pudding. "I don't know what I'm doing wrong."

"It happens to the best of us, dear." The corners of Doreen's eyes crinkled with amusement.

Harriet had begged for advice after making a flop of the ones she'd baked for Will last week in honor of the UK's national Yorkshire Pudding Day, celebrated on the first Sunday of February every year.

Doreen peeked at the batter Harriet was still whisking. "Don't worry. With my tips, your puds will retain all their puffed-up glory. First thing to remember is to chill your batter before baking."

Doreen's eleven-year-old son, Randy, raced into the kitchen. "Is supper almost ready?"

"Not for an hour. Did you boys make sure the gates were latched properly after you checked the flock?"

"Aye." Randy eyed the platter his mom was filling with pickles.

Lowering her voice, Doreen asked Harriet, "Did you hear that another three ewes went missing yesterday? From the Huckaby place this time." She tsked. "Farmers can never afford to lose stock. But to lose ewes in lamb in this economy…" Doreen shook her head. "And one of them was their blue-ribbon winner, no less. They're fortunate the entire flock didn't follow the trio out."

Harriet flinched. She'd visited the Huckaby farm yesterday morning. What if she'd been the one who failed to secure the gate properly? She'd promised herself that she'd double-check every gate she passed through after the Trussels' ram escaped soon after she'd attended that farm. And she'd warned her intern to do the same. But if she was second-guessing herself, her clients probably were too.

"No one has spotted the ewes wandering about?"

"Nay." Doreen shooed Randy away. "If you boys are done with your chores, go finish your board game with Ava and Ella. They should be done setting the dining room table by now."

"Okay." Randy snagged a pickle on his way out of the kitchen.

Harriet chuckled at Doreen's eye roll. "You must have to cook nonstop to keep your brood full." Doreen and her husband, Tom, had five children ranging in age from five to sixteen. And every time Harriet visited, the kitchen smelled divine, thanks to Doreen's baking expertise.

"I love it." Her friend's voice exuded joy. "But with our farm-tour plans for the school's half-term break, mealtimes will be crazier than ever around here."

The reminder of the lengths to which so many farmers had to go to keep their farms viable pricked Harriet with another dose of guilt. If she was responsible for costing the Huckaby family three of their best ewes, she'd also cost them the lambs the ewes were expecting. Shutting down the thought before her fretting spoiled her visit with Doreen, Harriet slid the bowl of batter into the fridge and turned her full attention to Doreen's explanation of their plans.

Harriet shook her head in wonder. Lambing was already a hectic time for sheep farmers. Adding educational entertainment for tourists to their to-do list was a huge undertaking. "Maybe I should feature you in the article I've been asked to write."

"Article for what?"

"An American veterinary magazine. I occasionally submitted pieces when I lived Stateside. Now that I'm practicing here, they've asked me to write something for their international feature. Usually, the articles contrast the veterinary practices of the featured country with the US. But I've proposed writing about how farmers are diversifying revenue streams to supplement their farm income."

"Is that so different than a Montana rancher converting his spread into a dude ranch? Or the B&Bs and 'glamping' cabins that farmers rent to tourists?"

"I suppose not." Harriet sighed. "I'd like to find a uniquely Yorkshire hook for my article though."

"I'll give it some thought and let you know if I come up with any ideas."

"Thank you." Harriet wiped down the counter where she'd been working. "By the way, the outdoor play area Tom built for the tourists looks great. The wash station is a fabulous addition. Will you allow visitors in with the newborn lambs?"

"No. We don't want to upset the new mamas. We usually have to hand-rear a dozen or so lambs every year, though, so in those cases, we might let visitors help bottle-feed them."

Harriet nodded. It wasn't uncommon for ewes with twins to not have enough milk.

"Besides seeing newborn lambs, the children can have a pony ride and pet and feed the goats, rabbits, and cow."

"Not the alpacas?" Harriet teased. Alpacas weren't always as amiable as they were cute, often seeing unfamiliar living things as a threat rather than a potential friend.

Doreen chuckled. "Tom built a second fence around the alpaca pen so young'uns can get close enough to admire them without touching them. Of course, if the littlest ones are anything like our Terrance, they'll be more interested in playing with the toy tractors in the big sandpit than anything else." She opened the oven door and checked the temperature of her roast beef then pricked a couple of potatoes and carrots with a fork. Seemingly satisfied, she removed the roasting pan from the oven. "Traditionally, we use pan drippings to bake our Yorkshire puds, but we'll save this for gravy and use lard tonight." She raised the oven temperature and retrieved a couple of muffin tins from the cupboard. "Add a half teaspoon of lard to each cup, then we'll put them in the oven to heat."

Harriet did as instructed while Doreen transferred her roasted vegetables to heated bowls and drained the pan drippings for gravy.

By the time the rest of the meal was sorted, the oven had reached the higher temperature, and Doreen set the muffin tins inside. "You want to heat the fat in your muffin tins until it's smoking hot before you add your batter."

Harriet cringed, remembering how, thanks to an emergency vet call, she'd once forgotten about her tins in the oven. Thankfully, the blaring smoke alarm alerted her before she'd made it out the door. This time, she kept a close eye on the situation. When Doreen agreed the fat was hot enough, Harriet quickly poured the chilled batter into each cup.

"Now"—Doreen dried her hands on a tea towel as Harriet closed the oven door—"don't open that door again until they're done, or your puds will sink."

"But how will I know when they're done if I can't look at them?" Harriet squinted through the oven's window, an option she didn't have with her grandad's old stove. But even with a window, it would be difficult to tell.

Doreen set the timer. "They should be done when this goes off. Ideally, we want to see at least a ten-centimeter rise and a golden-brown crispy exterior."

Harriet was still getting used to the metric system, but she remembered enough about conversions to know that ten centimeters translated to about four inches. "How do you keep them from sinking once you take them out of the oven?"

"Keep them away from drafts and serve them as soon as possible." Doreen patted Harriet's arm. "But don't sweat it if they collapse. They'll still taste great. We are home cooks, my dear. No one expects perfection or professionalism. If they did, they could go pay for it."

"We're here." Harriet's aunt Jinny, who lived in the dower cottage next to Harriet's house, came in the kitchen door.

"We?" Harriet tilted her head to peek past her aunt. Her uncle had passed away several years ago, and if Aunt Jinny had started dating, she hadn't breathed a word to Harriet.

Aunt Jinny ushered in their handsome pastor, Fitzwilliam Knight.

Harriet's heart jolted. She hadn't told anyone other than Polly and Aunt Jinny that she and Will had started dating. Well, tried to start. So far, they'd canceled more dates than they'd managed to keep, thanks to frequent veterinary or parishioner emergencies. Will had gamely accompanied her on a couple of farm calls that had usurped their plans, but offering to reciprocate on his emergency calls hadn't felt appropriate. If someone needed him, they usually required his discretion as well.

"I'd planned to invite Pastor Will to our Yorkshire Pudding Day celebration last week, but then Tom and I came down with that nasty cold the kids brought home from school," Doreen explained, clearly unaware that Will had celebrated the occasion—over thoroughly sorry puddings—with Harriet.

His hazel eyes twinkled. "I hear Harriet is tonight's guest cook in that department."

She smoothed the fine hairs around her face that had worked free of the braid she'd put in before starting. "Yes, and I hope your expectations aren't too high. I haven't yet managed to make a single batch that didn't sink."

Will laughed, a hearty, friendly sound that warmed Harriet to the tips of her toes. "My dad says they hold more gravy that way."

Will's good-natured response dispelled Harriet's nerves. Realizing she was standing there grinning at him like a starry-eyed schoolgirl, she busied herself cleaning the mixing bowl.

Terrance, Doreen's youngest boy, raced into the kitchen, almost knocking Aunt Jinny off her feet. "Dr. Bailey, Dad wants you to come quick."

Doreen squatted in front of her son and grasped his arms. "What's happened?"

"Missy is having her baby, but it's got too many legs."

Harriet had already shed her apron and grabbed her jacket from the back of the kitchen chair. There could be a couple of explanations for the child's statement, neither of them particularly good. "I'll see to it," she assured Doreen. "I'll leave you to make sure those Yorkshire puddings don't sink."

Harriet found Tom in the Danbys' maternity barn.

"Am I ever glad to see you," Tom said, the relief palpable in his voice. "She's got twins jostled about in there and near as I can tell, one is trying to push its leg out at the same time as the other's forelegs and head."

Harriet immediately crouched, heedless of her good trousers, next to the bawling ewe. She whispered reassurances to the distressed mama as she assessed the situation. "It's difficult to tell which leg belongs to which lamb."

Harriet managed to push back the head of the lamb that was determined to be first, enough to untangle its legs from those of its siblings. "Actually, she's carrying three lambs."

"Three?" Eager anticipation punctuated Tom's exclamation. "The young'uns will be happy about that. One to bottle-feed for sure. Our farm visitors will enjoy having a go at that too."

Finding the lamb's second leg folded between a sibling's forelegs, Harriet gently detangled it. Moments later, the lamb made its debut to the cheers of an audience, whose arrival Harriet hadn't been aware of until that moment. As Harriet wiped the little one's face, she spotted Doreen and Will. "How'd the puds come out?"

Doreen grinned. "As perfect as that lamb."

Will beamed at Harriet admiringly, and she felt heat creep into her face.

Pleased as punch, Harriet returned her attention to the next lamb. But the experienced mama didn't need any more help. Harriet remained at her side in case anything came up, but the rest of the delivery went smoothly.

Aunt Jinny donned her metaphorical physician's hat long enough to advise Doreen, "You might want to post signs outside the maternity barn advising expectant mums to mind where they go."

"Oh dear, yes. Thank you for the reminder. Your dad was always after me not to help with lambing or chores when I was pregnant."

Doreen's eldest daughter, thirteen-year-old Ava, snapped some photos of Harriet with the lambs. "These will be a hit on our social media. If that's okay with you, Dr. Bailey?"

"No problem."

"Be sure to tag Cobble Hill Veterinary Clinic," Will urged, shooting Harriet a wink.

Harriet's heart warmed at his thoughtfulness in ensuring that she might benefit from the advertising too. Thankfully, business had been steady over the past few weeks, and with lambing season almost upon them, she expected to be even busier. Although farmers were able to handle most complications, the sheer number of lambs due to be born in the area over the next three months meant there'd be more call for her specialized skills.

Harriet washed off as best she could with the bucket of warm soapy water Doreen's eldest son brought to her. "If it's okay with all of you, I'll zip home for a quick shower and change of clothes."

Despite living next door to the Danby farm, it was still more than half a mile from door to door, but thankfully she'd driven over. "I shouldn't be long."

"No problem. I'll keep everything warm until you return." Doreen herded her children toward the house, trailed by Will and Aunt Jinny.

Tom, who'd been trying to convince the ewe to take to all three of her lambs, finally conceded defeat and said he'd better fetch the wee one a bottle.

Harriet climbed into her ancient Land Rover. She still called it the Beast, although with a little more fondness than when she'd first arrived in White Church Bay. That had a lot to do with the fact that she'd grown adept at driving stick shift, even on the steep hills about the Yorkshire countryside.

She'd scarcely driven a few hundred yards when a fox bolted across the road in front of her.

She stamped on the clutch and the brake simultaneously and threw the stick into neutral.

The animal made it across unscathed. But when it paused and her headlights caught the glint of its eyes, she wasn't sure it was a fox. She squinted through the side window for a better view. The last thing farmers needed worrying their sheep was a stray dog. Unfortunately, whatever it was disappeared through the hedgerow.

She drove the remaining distance to the cliffside property she'd inherited from her grandfather. The traditionally thatched carriage house at the front held the Bailey Art Gallery, which showcased her grandad's paintings for curious tourists, while Cobble Hill Veterinary Clinic occupied a portion of the main floor of the two-story house that sat behind the gallery, with Aunt Jinny's dower cottage next to it. A big barn sat off on the far side of the property, which she used for large animals in her care and occasionally for boarding clients' pets.

Harriet parked and climbed out of the Beast, frowning when Maxwell's barks greeted her from inside the house. The dachshund, whose hindquarters were paralyzed, managed to dash around the main floor thanks to the wheeled prosthesis her grandfather had gotten for him. He usually didn't make much of a fuss over her arrival, since he was used to her coming and going from the clinic throughout the day.

Hurrying inside, she gave him a reassuring pat. "Hey, what's the matter, boy?"

The dog calmed and led the way to the kitchen, clearly anticipating a treat. A moment later, Charlie, Cobble Hill's resident calico, sauntered in to make sure she didn't miss out. Purring loudly, she batted her bowl ahead of Maxwell's. What she lacked in traditional cuteness, thanks to scars sustained in a fire as a kitten, she made up for in personality. Harriet didn't mind. After all, Charlie had to live up to her name. Grandad had called all of his office cats Charlie regardless of gender, saying that it gave him one less thing to remember.

Harriet humored the cat by adding the treats to her bowl first then gave Maxwell an extra one for chivalrously waiting his turn. Switching lights on as she went, Harriet dashed upstairs, grabbed a clean outfit, and hit the shower.

Right before she shut off the water, she heard Maxwell barking again. Grabbing a fluffy bath towel, she wrapped it around herself and opened the bathroom door. "Maxwell? What is it?"

The dog quieted, and a quick glance out the window confirmed no one had driven in. Harriet dried off and got dressed.

Again, she thought she heard Maxwell bark. *That sounds like an engine.* She hurried to a window that overlooked the parking area she shared with her aunt, but the Beast sat alone. Confused, she cocked her ear toward the hall. She could definitely hear an engine. It sounded as if it came from the rear of the property. Harriet hightailed it to a window on that side of the house. The field that stretched from Aunt Jinny's cottage to the public cliffside path and North Sea beyond was shrouded in darkness.

Her pulse skipped. *Anyone could be out there, and I wouldn't know.* Kids sometimes raced dirt bikes along the cliff path, even though they weren't supposed to. And she didn't want to think about the unwelcome intruders they'd had around the house and outbuildings the past few months.

"Get a grip," she scolded herself, pivoting to peer out a side window. Faint lights from the Danbys' place winked comfortingly. Maybe the engine noise was from Tom starting a tractor.

Annoyed with herself for wasting so much time searching for the source of a phantom sound, Harriet returned to the ensuite bathroom—and tripped over something with a shriek. She grabbed the bedpost to keep from falling. "Charlie, you've got to stop sneaking up on me like that. Have you been bothering Maxwell too? Was that why he barked?"

Charlie darted under the bed and swatted at Harriet's foot as she walked by. But ten seconds later, barking erupted again. Harriet again dashed to the window overlooking the car park.

This time a streak of red light crossed the drapes as she pushed them aside. But when she peered down, she couldn't see any vehicles. She ran to the front of the house in time to see the dust from a large van driving away.

Thinking she might have missed hearing an emergency call, she checked her phone for messages. Nothing. "It couldn't have been too urgent," she muttered to Charlie, heading for the stairs. "Otherwise, with the Beast parked outside and the lights on in the house, they would have waited longer for me to get to the door. Just as well. Everyone will be waiting for me at the Danbys'."

Once downstairs, Harriet scratched behind Max's ears. "You tried to get my attention, didn't you, boy? Not to worry. Whoever it was is gone now." She grabbed her coat and keys and headed out.

She slowed as her truck lights swept across the side of the art gallery. The engine she'd heard had sounded as if it came from behind the building.

She drove a quick loop around the gallery to the barn. Nothing was there now. And it was too dark to see footprints or tire treads.

But what if her impromptu return had surprised yet another intruder? And what had they been doing there in the first place?

CHAPTER TWO

Stars dotted the moonless sky as Harriet, Aunt Jinny, and Will left the Danbys' following their Sunday evening get-together. Stepping away from the light spilling from the front porch, Harriet tilted back her head. "The stars are so beautiful here."

"We are spoiled," Aunt Jinny agreed. "I didn't realize how little light pollution we had compared to most places until DarkSky International designated this area a Dark Sky Place. In fact, our annual Dark Skies Festival started this weekend."

"What does that mean?" Harriet asked.

"DarkSky International is committed to light pollution education and reduction around the world," Aunt Jinny explained. "Our Dark Skies Festival has tons of events to educate and celebrate the beauty of nights being dark."

"That reminds me," Will said. "There's an event tonight on the boardwalk in White Church Bay. Apparently, a local historian is going to tell a ghost story under the stars. Would the two of you like to go with me?"

"I'd better not." Aunt Jinny opened her car door. "I have to be at the hospital early tomorrow to see a patient. But you should go, Harriet. Someone from the historical society usually shares a story or two."

"Sounds like fun. Sure." Harriet smiled at Will. "I'll follow you to town, in case an emergency call comes in."

His acknowledging hand squeeze filled her with anticipation. But while following him in the Beast to the parsonage, she had too much time to think. She'd confided to Aunt Jinny last week that she enjoyed Will's company, and she suspected Aunt Jinny had given the early-morning excuse to give them a chance to spend time alone. Yet as drawn as Harriet felt toward Will, she couldn't help worrying about the fallout if whatever was developing between them went south.

Attending church could get awkward, for one.

At least they didn't work together like she had with her ex-fiancé. She had no intention of leaving *another* country to get away from an ex. Not that she'd left America because of Dustin Stewart, per se, but the breakup had made it easier to accept her grandad's generous bequest.

Banishing the pessimistic thoughts, Harriet reminded herself to take it one day—or one romantic, starry night—at a time.

Will parked ahead of Harriet in his driveway then opened her truck door.

Her stomach twirled at his touch. Although they'd held hands a few times, they hadn't yet done so in public. Truth be told, she couldn't help wondering if he'd been trying to avoid being seen as a "couple." She couldn't blame him. As a pastor, he was bound to come under closer scrutiny. It was human nature.

But when they crossed the street, Will rested his hand at the small of her back.

A car filled with rowdy teens swerved into a driveway a few houses from where they crossed the road.

Beside her, Will stiffened, and his hand fell to his side once more.

"What's wrong?"

Will peered toward the newcomers as the lads spilled out of the car. "Hopefully nothing." He quickened his pace then stopped at the end of the driveway where the boys had parked.

"Aye up, Pastor," one boy greeted with a wave.

Harriet scanned the faces of the lads and squirmed at the realization that all of them were sizing *her* up, rather than paying any mind to the pastor.

"Good evening," Will said. "Where were you boys tonight?"

"Just knocking about," the boy responded vaguely.

A teen in glasses, however, said, "Whitby," earning himself an elbow jab from a dark-haired guy who appeared older than the rest, maybe already twenty.

"Really? What was going on there?" Will didn't ask like an inquisitor. He sounded genuinely interested. The activity had obviously generated a camaraderie among the group.

"Nothing special," the elbow jabber said. "Why?"

Will chuckled. "Because it sounds as if you had a great time, and our youth group leader has been asking for activity ideas."

"Then you should have them check out the old abbey," the elbow jabber said. "They've got cool stuff about the Vikings there."

"That sounds interesting," Will said. "Did the rest of you like it?"

Half-hearted shrugs and a couple "Yeah, I guess," came back from the group.

"Well, good. I'll pass that on. Have a good night, boys."

"Night, Pastor," they chorused.

Will steered Harriet around the bend to begin their descent to the bay. "Did you get the impression they didn't actually go to the abbey?" she asked him.

"If they had, I'm sure they would've given more details about what they liked about it."

"Do you know the one who mentioned the abbey?" Harriet recognized a couple of the boys from church, but not all of them.

"The one who obviously didn't want us to know they'd been to Whitby? His name is Simon Boyes. He's had it rough. Peggy Abbott took him in when his mum died, since his dad wasn't in the picture. Simon settled down for a while but walked out as soon as he hit eighteen. He worked as an itinerant farm laborer for a time."

"And now?"

"He showed up hungry and broke on Peggy's doorstep a few days before Christmas and asked if he could stay with her again. She agreed. But he's twenty now and not quite as agreeable to the house rules. Peggy's concerned he'll be a bad influence on her son, Ian—the lad who first greeted me."

"That's tough. I admire Peggy's willingness to try to help him."

Will nodded. "She has the patience of Job. And I'm praying Simon doesn't blow this second chance to be a part of their family."

Harriet's foot caught on the edge of a paving stone on the steep hill, and Will clasped her elbow to steady her.

A little embarrassed, she murmured, "The streets seem darker than usual, don't you think?"

"The town council asked residents to draw their drapes and use as few lights as possible this evening. They've dimmed the street-lights to enhance the night-sky viewing."

"I'm surprised they decided to host the event in town. I would have thought they'd want to do it in a field outside of town, well away from streetlights."

White Church Bay consisted of two sections—the lower original section built into the cliff a couple centuries before with its colorful row houses connected by a maze of footpaths, and the upper section where the church and parsonage sat, with ordinary streets and homes more typical of the last century. The main street they were walking now connected the upper and lower sections by following a fissure from the top of the cliff to the bay.

"The view of the night sky over the water is breathtaking either way," Will said. "But I suspect this venue offers tourists an added incentive to spend the night in town."

"I noticed there have been fewer tourists about since Christmas." Her grandfather's art gallery was a popular stop for tourists exploring the area, but the traffic through the gallery in January had been negligible.

"Numbers will pick up again with the school break and the spring weather," Will said.

They reached the picnic area seconds before the lights around its perimeter were extinguished.

"Harriet, is that you?" Polly tugged on Harriet's sleeve. "I didn't know you were coming into town for this."

"Will invited me to join him."

"How lovely." Polly's voice held an encouraging lilt despite the fact her own former beau, Van Worthington, no longer stood by her side. He'd been hopelessly besotted with her, but his eagerness to formally seal their future together had petrified Polly. She'd turned down his marriage proposal, and the poor man had been devastated.

Not that Harriet believed for a second that Polly didn't love Van, given how much she'd been moping around the clinic since their breakup. Harriet hoped Van knew that, and thought that the time apart might give Polly the space she needed to sort out her true feelings.

"Dierdre is here somewhere too," Polly said.

"Who's Dierdre?" Will asked.

"Dierdre Shipley. She's a university student who's been interning at the clinic after classes and on weekends," Harriet explained. "She wants to be a vet and is eager to get as much field experience as she can. I can't believe I haven't mentioned her to you. She's super energetic and asks tons of great questions."

"Keeps you on your toes then?" Will quipped.

"As a matter of fact, she does, but it's as good for me as it is for her."

A short, stout man holding an electric candle called for everyone's attention.

"That's Ralph Newman," Will whispered close to Harriet's ear. "He's the town historian."

Ralph welcomed everyone then talked about the goals of dark sky reserves. "Not only do these reserves promote astronomy and conserve power, but they also help safeguard the natural balance of ecosystems, since so much wildlife depends on the darkness to survive. It even improves *our* health," he added. "Too much artificial light exposure at night wreaks havoc with our circadian rhythms, which can lead to sleep disorders that cause a host of other health problems."

"Not to mention that the night sky is beautiful to look at," called an elderly female voice from the crowd.

"Aye," Ralph agreed. "We are indeed fortunate to be able to regularly enjoy an unpolluted view of the stars here in White Church Bay."

Harriet leaned closer to Will and whispered, "When the clouds cooperate." England was known for its frequent rain, but thankfully the weather seemed to be in their favor tonight.

Next, an amateur astronomist from town explained to the group how to find the North Star and directed their attention to various constellations.

Finally, Ralph reclaimed everyone's attention for the evening's promised "ghost story."

But it wasn't about the ghost of a long-ago smuggler roaming the fabled tunnels beneath the lower part of town, as Harriet had expected. It was about a ghost dog.

"On cold dark nights," Ralph said, "some say the dog's barking can still be heard as he roams the moors in search of his master."

As if on cue, a long mournful howl erupted from the cliffs north of town in the direction of the Danby farm.

Will chuckled. "They timed that well."

"It was 1947," the historian continued, clearly relishing the atmosphere the dog's howl had lent his story. "And White Church Bay faced its harshest winter in more than a century."

Moors near White Church Bay
February 1947

Samuel pulled his hat low over his ears and wrapped his scarf around his face, leaving only a narrow slit to see through. "Come on, Shep, we need to check on the sheep." Snatching up a ball of twine, Samuel opened the farmhouse door. Icy snow blasted his face and coated the floor in the short time he took to step out and yank the door closed behind him. Within seconds, the dog disappeared in the driving snow.

Samuel tied one end of the twine to the porch rail and let the ball unwind as he made his way to the pasture. The wind was so strong he had to lean into it to stay upright. The house disappeared behind him, save for the dim gaslight shining in the front window. In every direction, all he could see was white. "Shep," he called.

The border collie barked, and Samuel followed the sound like a homing beacon. His beloved sheepdog knew his job, but in this weather, if he lost his bearings and steered any stragglers the wrong way, they could wind up worse off. He prayed the twine would be long enough to reach the three-sided run-in, because without the guide rope to follow, he didn't have much hope of finding his way home.

If the sheep knew what was good for them, they would be hunkered down in their shelter, waiting out the storm. He couldn't afford to lose a single one.

As he trudged through the deepening drifts, the twine ball shrank with every step. The stone wall surrounding the pasture materialized in front of him. He walked along it, searching for the gate, but he ran out of twine before reaching it. He tied the twine to a branch of gorse bush and, skimming his hand over the rocks, continued walking along the wall until he reached the gate. But even from there the shelter wasn't visible. He whistled for Shep.

Nothing.

Samuel tried again.

No response.

He wasn't sure the dog could hear his whistle over the raging winds. He tried again.

Like an actor appearing from behind a curtain, the dog burst through the blinding snow, barking wildly.

Samuel feared it meant the sheep weren't all in the shelter. But there was no way he could guide them there in this. He couldn't see five feet in front of his face. If the wind had picked up too quickly for them to find their way to the barn, hopefully they had taken refuge beneath the trees in the valley. There they should survive the night.

Their wool provided built-in insulation, and the lanolin in it kept moisture away from the skin. And he'd given them extra rations of hay this morning. Digesting all that food would generate heat.

"Let's go back inside, Shep. There's nothing more we can do tonight."

Ralph paused for dramatic effect. "Five feet of snow accumulated on the hills in record time that night, burying thousands of sheep."

A dog's mournful howl sounded again, and the crowd gasped as the silhouette of a limping dog appeared in a shaft of moonlight on the cliff over the bay.

"When the storm cleared," Ralph continued, "shepherds and their faithful dogs attempted to locate and rescue what sheep they could. No one knows what happened to Samuel Bishop in the weeks that followed that fateful night. A neighbor found his dog roaming the moors alone one afternoon, then found Samuel's home empty. Samuel was never seen or heard from again."

The dog on the cliff limped into the darkness once more.

"Wow," Harriet said to Ralph as he stepped down from the riser. "You staged that well." At his quizzical expression, she motioned to the cliff. "With the dog."

He chuckled. "I can't take credit for that. Merely serendipity. Or perhaps Bishop's ghost dog walks again." He gave a ghostly warble.

Shaking her head, Harriet pulled out her phone.

"Who are you calling?" Will asked.

"Rand Cromwell, the dog catcher, about an injured dog wandering on the cliff."

Will frowned. "I'd suggest we walk up there to see if we can find him ourselves, but the cliffside path is too dangerous in the dark."

"I was thinking the same thing." Harriet dialed Rand and filled him in on the situation. After they finished the call, she told Will, "He's posting the information on the village's social media and to their lost-pet email list. So, hopefully, come daylight, someone will spot the dog and bring him in."

"Good to hear," Will said.

Behind them, Harriet heard Ralph saying to someone, "At the time, there were rumors that Samuel Bishop was involved in a secret project for the war department, and some have speculated that foreign spies got to him."

Will nudged Harriet with his elbow. "Wouldn't that make an interesting hook for your article? 'Farmer Supplements Income by Spying for the Government.'"

"Hey, you might be onto something." Harriet tapped the idea into the notes app on her phone. "Since the war was over, I doubt Samuel was a spy. But the country was still facing a major food crisis, right?"

"True. Meat rationing didn't end until 1954, I believe."

"Perhaps he was experimenting with crossbreeds that would produce more meat."

"I know who you could ask," Polly chimed in. "Rowena Talbot's husband."

"He never admitted to being Secret Service, did he?" Will asked, referring to the husband of the kidnapped woman Harriet had found last year. They believed Rowena had been abducted because of her husband's mysterious work.

"No. But agents aren't allowed to admit they're agents, are they?" Harriet grinned at Polly. "Still, there's no harm in asking. The worst he can do is refuse."

CHAPTER THREE

Monday morning, Harriet lingered over her breakfast and morning coffee while surfing the internet for information on the legend of Samuel Bishop and his ghost dog.

At the clinic phone's trill, she shut her laptop and took her dishes to the sink. When the ringing continued, she ducked into the clinic and was surprised to find it empty. Snatching up the phone, she glanced out the window, certain she'd heard Polly's car drive in a while ago.

"Did the Fosters pick up Dusty early?" Polly blurted over the line before Harriet finished her greeting.

Harriet blinked. Dusty, named after his penchant for rolling in the soot his master cleared from their old log burner, was a regular boarder in the practice's kennels. Thanks to his excitability around little ones, the Fosters booked him in whenever their young grandchildren came for an extended visit. He was scheduled to stay until Wednesday. "Not that I know of. Why do you ask?"

"I'm in the barn, and Dusty's not here."

Harriet's heart jumped to her throat. "I'll be right there." She grabbed her coat and ran across the garden to the barn. Dusty had been happily secured in his kennel when she took him his supper before heading to the Danbys' place yesterday afternoon. But she hadn't thought to check on him again last night. She should have, especially after seeing that dog limping along the cliff path. What would she tell Mr. and Mrs. Foster if she'd lost their dog?

Many of the dogs they boarded stayed in the house with her. Unfortunately, Dusty didn't get along with Charlie, so he stayed in the barn's kennels.

Polly met Harriet at the barn door, her face pale. "I've searched every nook and cranny. He's gone."

"Was the gate open?"

"No. See for yourself." Polly pointed to a pile of dirt in a far corner of the fenced yard that Dusty could access from the barn. "He must've dug his way out."

"The little sneak." Harriet called Rand to let him know the dog she'd reported seeing the night before could be their escapee. "It's a Shiba Inu. A medium-size dog, fairly friendly, but not so good with youngsters or cats."

"A Shiba Inu. That's the breed that resembles a fox, right?" Rand asked.

"Yes." Remembering the "fox" that had run in front of her car last night, Harriet gulped. She could kick herself for not realizing it might have been Dusty. If she had, she could have snagged him then before he hurt himself. Then again, she'd had no reason to think it might be him. After all, she'd thought he was secure in the kennels.

"Let's hope he hasn't picked up the scent of any newborn lambs," Rand said. "Shiba Inus have a high prey drive."

Harriet winced at the thought of the trouble Dusty might get himself into. Or might have already gotten himself into. Possibly leaving a farm gate improperly latched was bad enough. Being responsible for the escape of a potential lamb killer was unforgivable. After hanging up with Rand, Harriet said to Polly, "I hate to say this, but I hope the limping dog we spotted last night was Dusty."

"I was thinking the same thing. At least the injury would slow him down and hopefully keep him from getting into any trouble."

"How much time before our first appointment?"

Polly checked her watch. "About twenty minutes. We'd better get back to the clinic." She hurried ahead. "Should I call the Fosters and let them know what's going on?"

Harriet scanned the ground. "Let's hold off a few hours. I'll see if I can spot his tracks. The Fosters planned to take their grandchildren to an ice festival today. I don't want to spoil their day out."

Harriet found paw prints in the soft dirt on the other side of the fence but nothing beyond its immediate vicinity. She jogged to the road where she'd seen her supposed fox cross and scanned the field beyond the hedgerow, but she couldn't see any clue as to where he might have gone after disappearing through it. If the animal she'd seen before supper was the same one they'd seen on the cliff, he would have had to cross over the road again at some point.

Everything in her wanted to get out and search, but a text from Polly alerted her to the arrival of her first client. Sighing, Harriet jogged back to the house. If the school's half-term break were this week, she could enlist the help of the Danby children to hunt for Dusty.

"Good news," Polly announced as Harriet stepped through the clinic door. "Will found the limping dog we saw last night. From his description, it's gotta be Dusty."

Harriet melted with relief. "That's wonderful."

"He's bringing him in now."

"Okay, I'll examine him here, and then we'll have to keep him inside until we can secure the kennels."

"No worries. I'll get a crate ready for him." Polly motioned to the exam room. "Meanwhile, your first patient is waiting for you."

Thankfully, the first patient was Chief, an Alsatian in for a routine checkup and vaccination. By the time Chief sauntered out with the biscuit she'd given him for being a star patient, Will arrived with Dusty.

Harriet hurried to the pair. "How did you find him?" she asked.

"I couldn't stop thinking about the poor thing limping about the moors in the cold and dark, so I went out at first light," Will explained. His tender heart for animals as well as humans was one of the many things that attracted Harriet to him. "I started up the cliffside path toward where we'd seen him and eventually found him holed up under the bushes along one of the stone walls."

"We'll have to let Rand know he's been found," Harriet said to Polly.

"I already did," Will said. "He's the one who told me you were missing a dog."

"I can't thank you enough for finding him." Harriet squatted beside the dog and examined the leg he was favoring. "I feel so horrible that I didn't check on him before bed last night. I think I might've even seen him run across the road when I returned to the house before supper, but I mistook him for a fox. I never imagined he could get out. We've taken such great care to keep the barn area secure."

"Don't beat yourself up. He's safe. And I think the limp is due to a thorn. I pulled it out, but you might want to disinfect his paw."

Harriet pushed to her feet. "I'll do that." Overwhelmed with gratitude, she hugged Will without noticing who might be in the waiting room. Blushing at the thought of what people might think, she drew back. Happily, their only audience was her grinning receptionist.

"My pleasure," Will assured her, beaming. "But I'm afraid I need to dash. I have a meeting. I'll call you later if I can." He hurried out of the clinic.

Smiling, Harriet led Dusty to the exam room and soon confirmed Will's assessment. "Well, young man, I hope you've learned your lesson and are going to behave yourself now."

He wagged his tail and licked her hand.

"I forgive you." She tousled his fur. "But that doesn't mean I'm ready to trust you. I'm afraid you'll have to stay inside with us for a while."

He sniffed at her pocket, and she gave him a treat. "Let's go. Polly will get you settled. I have other patients to see." To Polly, Harriet said, "Could you please call Mike Dane and ask him to reinforce the dog run as soon as possible? Hopefully, he isn't in the middle of a major project for someone else. I doubt Dusty will be content to stay inside for long."

"I'll call Mike straight away. I'm sure he'll find a way to fit us in even if he's busy. Handymen are used to juggling emergency calls. Although after Dusty's adventure, I suspect he'll be happy to sleep the rest of the day."

The next time Harriet checked on Dusty, he was sound asleep in his crate, as Polly had predicted.

Thanks to a free last period that allowed Dierdre to leave school early, she arrived shortly after two o'clock to assist with the remaining afternoon appointments. Her flaming red hair was tied in a ponytail that bobbed as she walked, and she exuded an enthusiasm Harriet wished she could bottle.

When Harriet and Dierdre collected their last patient from the waiting room an hour later, Polly held her hand over the office phone's mouthpiece. "You have a farm emergency at Hollyhock Hollow Farm—the Mitchells."

"How much of an emergency?"

"It's a sheep showing signs of bluetongue virus."

Harriet groaned. "Tell them I'll be there as soon as I can." She sincerely hoped they weren't facing a case of bluetongue. Given its high mortality rate in sheep, an outbreak of the disease at the onset of lambing season could be devastating.

"Isn't bluetongue spread by midges?" Dierdre asked as they led Mr. Slazenger and his cat, Tabbytha, to the exam room.

"Yes," Harriet confirmed.

"But midges don't come out until May," Dierdre reasoned. "So if they're the disease vector, it's doubtful we'd see a case crop up this time of year, isn't it?"

Harriet smiled at the technical jargon Dierdre had adopted.

"Actually," Mr. Slazenger interjected, "when we have a warm winter, midges can come early. I had some pestering me this morning on my walk."

"Are you sure they were midges?" Dierdre swiped her thumb across her phone screen, apparently planning to see if the UK could have midges in February.

By the time Harriet finished Tabbytha's checkup, Dierdre had confirmed Mr. Slazenger's statement.

Dierdre shivered. "I can't believe they're out already. I hate those things."

"I agree." Harriet handed Tabbytha to her owner. "She's in great shape, Mr. Slazenger. Since she's approaching ten years old, you may see some signs that she's slowing down. Let me know if you notice anything concerning, but I don't see any reason why she shouldn't have many happy years ahead of her yet."

"Thanks, Doc."

Harriet collected the address for Hollyhock Hollow Farm while Mr. Slazenger settled his bill with Polly in reception. "Did you bring your wellies?" Harriet asked Dierdre as they headed out to the Land Rover.

"They're in the boot." Dierdre dashed to the trunk of her car and pulled out a gleaming pair of rubber boots. "I cleaned them before I packed them so I wouldn't carry any pathogens from one farm to the next. I was at my boyfriend's farm last weekend, and he's totally obsessive about that sort of thing."

"Hosing off and disinfecting your boots between farm calls is a great habit to get into." Harriet climbed into the truck and waited for Dierdre to buckle up. "The number of ways a vet can carry an infection from one farm to the next is quite staggering."

"Reggie—Reggie Springfield, my boyfriend—says a vet's car keys can even do that."

"That's a new one on me. We all wash our hands after examinations."

"Sure, but he says not everyone uses a scrub brush to clean their nails. Or even if they do, they'll carry their equipment and medicine or sample bottles barehanded, all of which could've picked up contamination in the barn or pasture."

"That's true," Harriet conceded. "It sounds as if your boyfriend has given you lots of good points to remember."

Dierdre chuckled. "Like I said, he's totally obsessive. But it's probably because his grandfather never fully recovered his stock after the foot-and-mouth epidemic back in 2001."

"I remember that." Harriet's thoughts hearkened to her childhood. "We were planning a trip to the UK for the summer when the epidemic hit, but as it spread, Grandad asked us not to come. No one was leaving their farms unless it was absolutely necessary, for fear of carrying the disease back with them. My grandad said it wasn't so much the financial losses but sheer grief over losing their animals that shook many farmers to their core."

"And restocking wasn't as simple as going to an auction and buying replacements," Dierdre added.

"I imagine there wasn't much for sale with the entire country's livestock depleted as it was."

"Reggie's grandfather had what's called 'hefted' sheep. They could graze on communal land on the moors because they had been reared there and knew where they belonged without fences. Just like everyone else, he had to rebuild his stock from what little remained."

"So he had to keep every new lamb rather than the best of them," Harriet surmised, "meaning the quality of his stock would have suffered."

"That's why Reggie's family is working so hard to rebuild the flock's quality. But it's tough."

"It takes a special breed of people to stick with farming through all of that. I'm praying this farm call won't prove to be something as devastating as that."

They arrived at the small holding a few minutes later. Harriet had never been to the farm before, so when no one came out to meet her, she knocked at the house.

A petite woman attempting to rein in three young children opened the front door and spoke through the screen. "Are you the vet?"

"That's right. I'm here to see a sick ewe. Are you Mrs. Mitchell?"

"I'm her sister, Rina. I hope I was right to call. I'm minding the farm and children so my sister and her husband can have a bit of a holiday. They haven't had a night away since the triplets were born three years ago."

Remembering the Danbys' new four-legged triplets, Harriet smiled. It was nice to see blessings coming in threes. Although she imagined the youngsters got into their fair share of trouble. "Don't worry about bundling up the children. I can find my own way. Is the ewe in the barn, or the field?"

"In the first pasture next to the drive. She's due to lamb next month. So when I saw her tongue this morning…" The frazzled woman shook her head. "I didn't want to worry my sister and spoil their holiday, but I didn't think I should wait to have her checked if it's something catching. There was so much talk about that nasty bluetongue virus a couple of years ago."

"You did the right thing to call, though bluetongue isn't actually contagious between animals. However, if there are infected midges around, that's another story," Harriet said. "I'll go see what we're dealing with."

She left the house and poked about in the barn until she found a stash of grain. After filling a bucket, she led Dierdre into the pasture.

"Reggie's sheep come when he claps," Dierdre said.

"Probably because he follows up with treats." Harriet jiggled the grain bucket, and the ewes stampeded toward them. Checking each one's mouth while they dodged one another for grain proved to be more challenging.

"Here she is," Dierdre announced.

"Well done. Hold her against your legs if you would." Harriet took the ewe's temperature first. "Normal. That's a good sign. Animals infected with BTV usually present with fever and blisters besides the telltale blue tongue and lips." Harriet moved to the ewe's head. "Her eyes and ears are clear. And her lips are still pink." With a little effort, Harriet managed to coax open the ewe's mouth. "Wow, that's certainly a different-color tongue. Although more on the purple side than blue." Tilting her head, Harriet examined the sheep's teeth and laughed. "And I'm pretty sure BTV doesn't turn teeth blue."

Dierdre shot her a flabbergasted look.

Harriet took over holding the sheep. "Check it out. I suspect Rina saw the discolored tongue and assumed the worst."

Dierdre peered into the ewe's mouth and shook her head. "You think one of those little scamps fed her colored candy or something?"

"That's my guess." Harriet made a note on her phone of the ewe's ear tag number. "Let's go have another chat with the auntie."

Seeing the panic in Rina's eyes as they stood outside the screen door, Harriet pitied the poor woman, who clearly hadn't realized the challenge she'd face in offering her sister a much-needed break. "Good news," Harriet announced to alleviate Rina's concern. "I didn't detect anything worrying. Did the children happen to give the ewes any treats this morning?"

"Yes, we took them a few apple slices. That's okay, isn't it? My sister said they sometimes feed them carrots or apples."

"Absolutely. And what about candy? Or blueberries, perhaps?"

The woman's eyes widened. Then her gaze shot to the cherub-faced boy galloping around the entranceway on a hobby horse. "Nathaniel Mitchell, did you feed your blueberries to Matilda?"

The boy grinned at her, baring purply-blue-tinged teeth. "She likes them."

Shaking her head, Rina returned her attention to Harriet. "I'm so sorry for wasting your time."

"It's all right. I'm glad it was nothing serious, and I prefer conscientious clients who call me for nothing to those who ignore something serious."

A boy identical to Nathanial except for his different color T-shirt pushed past his aunt's legs. "For vet." He held up a picture of a big blue cloud with four lines radiating from its bottom half. A stick figure stood beside it consisting of a large smiling head and two legs—no arms or body. Harriet guessed it was supposed to be a picture of herself caring for the much-loved Matilda.

"That's adorable," Dierdre gushed.

Rina opened the screen door so the boy could give Harriet the picture.

His grin melted Harriet's heart. She crouched to his level. "Thank you for this lovely picture. What's your name?"

He ducked his head shyly and hid behind his aunt's legs.

"Ned," Rina answered for him.

Rising, Harriet said, "No need to worry your sister and her husband about a vet bill. We'll call Ned's sketch even payment for today's call. I might even hang it in the children's room of my grandfather's art gallery."

Rina gasped. "That's so kind of you."

"Have a good day." Harriet fluttered her fingers in farewell to the youngsters and then headed to her truck with Dierdre.

"Do you often do freebies?" Dierdre asked.

"I don't make a habit of it, or else I wouldn't eat. But Grandad sometimes took barter in lieu of money, so sometimes I do too."

Twenty minutes later, they arrived at Cobble Hill as Polly was locking up the clinic. "I'm so glad you got back before I left. Doreen called. Their tup Prince Charming is missing." *Tup* was the locals' word for a ram.

"Missing? As in escaped?" Harriet stepped sideways to a vantage point that allowed her to scan the Danbys' pasture wall bordering Cobble Hill Farm. The ram had a reputation for being a character, but it had never been an escape artist.

"There's a section of disturbed hedgerow where they think he pushed through."

Harriet chewed her bottom lip as her gaze strayed to the barn where Dusty should have been last night—and hadn't been. "When was the last time the Danbys saw Charming?"

"The boys saw him Sunday afternoon."

Around when Dusty went AWOL. The Shiba Inu was about a fourth of the missing ram's size, but Harriet wouldn't put it past him to try chasing something that large. "Do they know how Charming got out?"

"They're not sure. They couldn't spot any useful tracks." Polly lowered her voice, her thoughts clearly mirroring Harriet's. "Though there were paw prints in places."

"Dog prints? If a dog got into the pasture, it could be a case of sheep worrying," Dierdre speculated. "Does a public path run through their field?"

"No." *But that doesn't mean a dog didn't get in there.* Harriet clamped her mouth shut, not wanting to blame Dusty without proof. If he'd taken to sheep worrying and had developed a talent for escaping, they certainly wouldn't be able to kennel him at the clinic again.

After all that Doreen had done to make Harriet feel welcome here, Harriet's heart wrenched at the prospect of admitting that the disappearance of the prizewinning ram was her fault.

She had to find Prince Charming before it was too late.

CHAPTER FOUR

The dark gray clouds hovering over Cobble Hill Farm suddenly felt like a foreboding portent.

"Is Dusty still inside?" Harriet asked Polly, fearing he might try to run away again even if Mike had figured out a way to stop him from digging escape tunnels.

"He is," Polly confirmed. "I gave him supper and walked him around the garden before crating him again. Mike is burying chicken wire around the base of the fence to keep him from digging his way out. I didn't think you'd want to risk putting Dusty back in the barn until that's finished."

"You're right. Thank you." When she'd examined the dog earlier, Harriet hadn't seen any signs that he'd attacked another animal. But if they found Prince Charming bleeding on the moors from bite wounds, the timing of Dusty's escape would be too coincidental for him not to be their chief suspect. Harriet felt sick. First Huckaby's prize ewes disappeared after she might have failed to properly latch their gate, and now this.

"My brother, Tristan, has a well-trained sheep dog." Dierdre pulled her phone from her pocket. "I could ask him to bring it here to help us search."

"That would be wonderful. Thank you so much." Harriet prayed they'd find Prince Charming uninjured. Then, as tempted as she was to put off calling her neighbor, Harriet went into her office to do so while Dierdre waited outside for her brother.

At Doreen's harried-sounding "hello," a fresh wave of guilt swamped Harriet. "Polly told me about Prince Charming. Is there any sign your other sheep have been distressed?"

"No. Thank goodness, because all our pregnant mamas who are due within the next few weeks were in the same fold with him."

"I'm glad to hear it. I asked because a dog I'm boarding got loose Sunday afternoon and I'm afraid he could have been responsible." Harriet's voice cracked with emotion. "I feel terrible."

Doreen remained silent for what felt like an eternity. Finally, she said, "I appreciate you letting me know. But honestly, I doubt a dog was to blame. Tom was in the barn half the night taking care of the littlest lamb you delivered of those triplets. He would've heard the dog barking if it had gone after the sheep."

Harriet wasn't sure how true Doreen's assumption was. Dogs barked in the countryside all the time, usually about nothing worth paying attention to. Tom might have heard a dog barking and ignored it, assuming it was coming from somewhere else. Or a dog chasing prey might not have barked at all.

"In fact, I doubt he wandered off after dark. Sheep tend to stay rooted to whatever spot they're in once the sun goes down."

Harriet appreciated Doreen's attempts to assuage the guilt she felt, but the paw prints in the field told another story. "My intern is seeing if her brother can come by with his herding dog, and we're going to search the area."

"Thank you. Tom checked with all the closest neighbors. He'd still be out there if he could. But with the sheep so close to lambing, we dare not leave them unattended."

"I understand." Plenty of ewes gave birth without help, but wise shepherds kept a close eye on their flocks for signs of trouble. Timely intervention could resolve most problems that might otherwise end in tragedy.

Harriet checked on Dusty, unable to fathom what might have inspired his flight. He'd never shown the slightest inclination to run away during previous stays. Sighing, she slipped a dog treat into his crate. "Until we find Prince Charming, I'm afraid you and I are both in the doghouse."

She changed into hiking boots and rejoined Dierdre outside as a beat-up black van pulled into the driveway. The noisy engine reminded Harriet of the sound she'd heard coming from the field last night and the vehicle she'd seen at the end of the driveway.

What if someone accessed the Danbys' pasture from her field to steal the ram? It could explain why Dusty dug his way out. Perhaps he was trying to defend the property.

She grimaced. An opportunist would have gone for a more easily accessible ewe from a pasture bordering a quiet road. Perhaps even a pregnant one if the thief wanted to score two for one. The three ewes who had disappeared Saturday had all been pregnant.

A sudden glimmer of hope that she wasn't responsible for any of their disappearances lightened her spirits, but she instantly tamped down the notion. Would she seriously rather have sheep rustlers roaming the countryside than have the disappearances be her fault?

But the burly man staring at her from the van's driver's seat was intimidating enough to be a rustler. She shivered at his icy glare. He certainly didn't appear as game to search the hills for missing sheep as Dierdre claimed. "Are you sure your brother is okay with doing this?" Harriet asked Dierdre.

"That's not my brother driving. That's Tristan's friend."

"Oh." The van's heavily tinted side windows prevented Harriet from seeing anyone else.

"They met at a sheepdog trial last fall."

"Really? He doesn't strike me as the type who'd be into working with dogs."

"I don't think he is. At least, I've never seen him with one."

The side door slid open, and a lanky guy and his dog jumped out.

"That's Tristan," Dierdre clarified.

The instant Tristan closed the door, the driver spun the vehicle around and screeched off.

Dierdre made a face at her brother. "He's real friendly, isn't he?"

"He's okay," Tristan protested.

After making introductions, they wasted no time getting started. Harriet and Dierdre trailed Tristan and his energetic border collie, Bouncer, through the fields, starting along the public pathway in the pasture adjacent to Cobble Hill.

"At least there isn't a railroad track around here," Dierdre said. "One runs close to where Reggie lives with his grandfather. When Reggie was younger, some new sheep his grandfather brought in wandered onto the tracks."

"The train whistle didn't scare them away?"

"No. The sheep wouldn't move for love or money. Just bleated when the conductor blew the train whistle. His grandfather didn't even know the sheep were missing until a neighbor heard about the train delay on the radio and phoned him."

"With any luck, an equally helpful neighbor will soon spot Prince Charming," Harriet said, trying to stay positive.

"Something could have spooked him," Dierdre said.

"In that case, he might've run straight off the cliff," Tristan said. "It wouldn't be the first time that's happened."

"I'm sure he'll turn up in someone's pasture," Dierdre said. "I'll mention his disappearance at the farmers' meeting I'm attending with Reggie on Thursday night."

"Goodness, I hope we find him before then," Harriet said. "It's a good idea though. I'll alert my clients to be on the lookout too."

"There is the odd unscrupulous farmer who wouldn't be above adding a wanderer to his own herd," Tristan pointed out.

"Surely not." Harriet couldn't imagine any of the local farmers stooping that low.

"Was his fleece painted?" Tristan asked.

Harriet called to mind the last time she'd seen the ram. "No, I don't think so. Only the ewes were painted, according to when they're due and with how many lambs."

"So another farmer could put his own mark on the ram and hide him in plain sight."

"That's awful," Dierdre said.

Tristan shrugged. "It happens."

Shielding her eyes from the setting sun, Harriet scanned the distant fields. She'd have to pay more attention to sheep markings as she drove about the countryside.

Tristan crossed into the next field. "Good thing the tup was a Suffolk and not a Shetland. A fellow I know had a Shetland that got twenty miles away before they caught up to it."

"That's crazy," Harriet said. "You'd think most sheep would stop at the next patch of green grass they found."

"But the grass has scarcely started to green up yet," Dierdre pointed out.

After more than an hour of searching, Harriet squinted toward the sinking sun. "We'd better head in."

"That'll do," Tristan called to Bouncer, who immediately broke off his search and came to heel.

Once they reached Cobble Hill, Dierdre opened the back door of her compact hatchback for Bouncer. "I'll ask my friends who bus in from north of town to watch for Prince Charming."

"That's great. Thank you both for everything."

Dierdre climbed into the driver's seat, and her brother swung in on the passenger side. "No problem. I'll see you tomorrow."

Seeing that Mike's truck was gone, Harriet relocated Dusty to his newly secured kennel in the barn before eating leftovers for supper. Since she couldn't do anything more about the missing ram until morning, she went to her grandfather's office to brainstorm ideas for the magazine article. The due date would arrive before she knew it. If she wanted the piece to be more than a one-off now that she'd left the States, she needed to make it extra special.

Springboarding from Samuel's story should do the job, especially if there was any truth to the theory she'd overheard Ralph talking about, regarding a secret government project. But she needed more than hints and theories to go on. She surfed the internet for information on government breeding schemes, particularly any from the 1940s that Samuel might have taken part in.

At first, she found little of use and began to rethink how else she might use Samuel's story as a hook. Given the recent bluetongue virus scare and ongoing fears of the next big epidemic that might wipe out a herd, perhaps she should explore the angle of how attached farmers get to their animals, especially those on small holdings.

She picked up her pen and began to write.

Yorkshire farmer Samuel Bishop seems to have died of a broken heart after losing his flock to a freak snowstorm in 1947. Given the cruelty of pestilence, disease, and harsh weather, his experience wasn't the first and surely won't be the last.

Frowning, Harriet chewed on the end of her pen. Talk about melodramatic. And for all she knew, it was complete fiction.

A spy angle would definitely be more intriguing.

She returned her focus to her online search and learned that England was seen as a world leader with its breeding programs. But if she wanted to use Samuel Bishop's story as the article's hook, she needed proof that he had been working on a government project when he disappeared.

Maybe she could learn more at the farmers' meeting Dierdre had mentioned. Most farms were passed down from generation to generation. And if farmers were as meticulous at record keeping as her grandfather and great-grandfather had been, one of them might still have journals from Samuel's day. She made a note in her phone to check the library's historical records.

Tuesday afternoon, Harriet called her next patient to the exam room a moment before Dierdre burst through the clinic door.

"Where's the fire?" Polly asked.

Dierdre gulped in a breath. "I think I might know where to find your neighbor's tup."

Harriet stopped in her tracks and motioned to her client to take her cat into the examination room, promising to join them momentarily. Then she met Dierdre at Polly's desk. "Where?"

"At Wilcox's Wanderings," Dierdre blurted.

"Shh." Harriet glanced at the exam room's open door. "What makes you think so? I'm sure the Danbys would've called there. And we searched one of his pastures last night."

"Last year, Wilcox's Wanderings made a killing with their half-term sheep farming events. Remember?"

"Actually, no, I was still in the US this time last year."

"Oh, right. Well, they did. They were the first farm in the area to have anything like that, and it was a huge hit. Families came from all over once those pictures of children cuddling lambs and bunnies went viral on social media."

"I remember," Polly agreed. "You thought we had lots of tourists at the gallery last August? That was nothing compared to the Wilcox event. Attendees caused a traffic jam on the road."

"But what does any of that have to do with Prince Charming?" Harriet pressed, hyperaware of the client waiting in her exam room.

"Think about it," Dierdre insisted. "The Danbys live less than two miles from the Wilcoxes. And closer to town. The Wilcoxes must be worried that the Danbys' half-term festivities will cut into their profits."

"But again, where does Prince Charming come into it?"

"Motive, means, opportunity." Dierdre ticked them off on her fingers. "The motive could be that they begrudge the Danbys horning in on their cash cow."

Polly gasped. "I'm sure Doreen mentioned something about having a special pen to show off their blue-ribbon winners from last year's agricultural show."

"There you go," Dierdre continued. "Mr. Wilcox likely hoped that losing one of their best animals would derail their plans."

Polly nodded. "I went to school with one of the Wilcox girls. "She was always pretty full of herself."

"Means and opportunity are easy," Dierdre went on. "Living so close, they'd be able to monitor the Danbys' comings and goings then move in and take the tup without anyone questioning what they were doing in the neighborhood."

Harriet wasn't convinced, but they did have to follow every lead. "Maybe we could pay the Wilcoxes a friendly visit once we're finished for the day. Right now, one of our patients is waiting for her vaccinations. Care to join me?"

Grinning, Dierdre shed her coat. "Absolutely."

Harriet instructed Dierdre on taking a patient history and anomalies to watch for during routine checkups. The young woman was a quick learner and brimmed with insightful questions. In the weeks since she'd begun helping Harriet, several pet owners had remarked on her curiosity with comments such as, "I've always wondered that myself."

As the last client exited with his Great Dane, Harriet patted Dierdre's back. "Good work. Your questions ignite a welcome curiosity in our pet owners. I must admit you've inspired me to offer better explanations of what I'm checking for and why during examinations. I think the enhanced dialogue has inspired at least some of our clients to be more attuned to what changes in their pet's behavior could mean."

Dierdre blushed under the praise. "My mum teases me about how many questions I've asked from the minute I could say *why*. She says she doesn't know how she would've survived without the internet on her cell phone everywhere we went."

Harriet laughed. "It seems that's how we all feel these days."

"Dad says we're bombarded with too much information—a lot of it questionable. 'Wolves in sheep's clothing,' he calls it. He quizzes my brother and me about things he's read to test our discernment."

"Good for him. More parents need to do that," Harriet said. "We all do. Doctors and vets see a lot of clients doling out tons of money on the latest 'miracle cure' they saw online somewhere."

"I know the ones you mean. They seem to have a lot of statistics to back them up. But if you read the studies they say support their claims, you discover they don't actually prove anything about what they're peddling."

"Exactly," Harriet agreed, impressed by Dierdre's astuteness. "I read—"

"I hate to interrupt," Polly said, coming into the exam room, "but an emergency call came in during your last appointment. A lame pony with a hot hoof at the Fairburn Farm."

Dierdre shot Harriet a worried frown. "We're still going to poke around Wilcox's Wanderings though, aren't we?"

Harriet's stomach churned at the teen's eagerness. As much as she wanted to find the missing ram, she hated to think any of her neighbors could be a thief. And if Wilcox was, how would he react to their snooping around and asking questions?

Not well, if she had to guess.

CHAPTER FIVE

While driving to the Fairburn farm, Harriet told Dierdre about the article she'd been asked to write and the idea of using the dog ghost story as a hook. "Or the story behind the story, I guess I should say. I'm thinking that if Samuel Bishop was working for the government, then it's possible he was commissioned to come up with a more robust breed of sheep to mitigate the food crisis of the time."

"You should talk to Reggie. He's been working on strengthening his grandfather's flock through crossbreeding. He reads everything he can on the subject and keeps amazing records on every detail, from feed types to how many days of sunshine they get."

"Sounds like a hardcore researcher himself."

"He's speaking at the farmers association meeting this week about his research," Dierdre said, pride evident in her voice. "That's why I'm going. You could come and listen in, if you want."

Attending the meeting might also be an excellent opportunity to meet other farmers Harriet could profile in her article. "If I don't have any emergencies, I'll try to do that."

When they neared the lane to the Fairburn farm, Dierdre sat forward and squinted out the window. "Could you slow down? I think that's Tristan."

As Harriet slowed the Beast, a border collie also came into view beside the lanky lad wearing a dark hooded jacket. "It looks like him," she said.

"What on earth is he doing here?"

"Maybe he's out for a hike with Bouncer. Do you want me to stop?"

"No, that's okay. I thought he had contract milking to do. I must've gotten it mixed up, because he's super conscientious. He wouldn't show up late for evening milking."

"I don't mind stopping to ask him about it," Harriet assured her.

"No, it's fine. Honestly."

Harriet turned onto the Fairburns' road, and a young girl sprinted up the driveway waving her arms. When she drew level with her, Harriet braked and lowered the window.

"Are you the vet?" the girl asked breathlessly.

"I am."

"It's my pony you've come to see."

"Then you'd better climb in and show me where it is."

The girl jumped in the back, her words tumbling over each other. "Her hoof's been hot since lunchtime, Mum says, and she doesn't want to walk." The girl pointed to a barn. "That way."

Harriet parked at the barn, and the girl burst from the vehicle, disappearing inside before Harriet had even unbuckled. Harriet and Dierdre gathered their supplies and followed her in.

They found the pony in a brightly lit, meticulously clean stall bedded with sweet-smelling straw. While Dierdre took notes, Harriet examined the pony and cataloged the symptoms. "The hoof is definitely hot to the touch. Note that it's been hot since lunchtime,

Dierdre." Harriet fitted her stethoscope into her ears and listened to the pony's heart, which sounded fast. "What's your name?" she asked the pony's owner.

"Tanya," the girl said.

"Tanya, could you please try to lead your pony a few steps so I can check out her gait?"

The girl sprang into action, but the obstinate pony refused to cooperate.

"That's okay," Harriet assured her. "I'm confident she has laminitis."

"What's that?" Tanya's voice quavered.

"Basically, she has severe inflammation in her front hoof. I'm going to take a couple of pictures to see how severe." Harriet turned to Dierdre. "Could you fetch the portable radiograph, please?"

"Sure thing." Dierdre returned a moment later, and Harriet showed her and Tanya how the machine worked.

The image that appeared confirmed her diagnosis. "Thankfully, your parents called me in right away. Because your pony is still young, we have a good chance of clearing this up for her." Harriet handed Tanya a pamphlet of instructions on how to care for the pony's laminitis then prepared an injection. "I'm going to give her something for the pain. I'll return tomorrow to assess her improvement, okay?"

Tanya's mom joined them and wrapped her arm around her daughter's shoulders. "Yes, do whatever she needs."

Dierdre distracted Tanya and her mother from the injection by asking about their sheep—the breeds, how many lambs they were expecting, how lambing usually went, and so on. The strategy worked, as Mrs. Fairburn boasted about their success in crossing Texels with Swaledales to produce a hardy cross with both desirable fleece and above-average muscle size, as well as their venture in building a herd of Border Leicesters.

By the time Harriet had packed the equipment into the Beast and scheduled a follow-up assessment for the next morning, the pony's discomfort already appeared to have lessened.

"Thank you for coming so quickly," Mrs. Fairburn said as Harriet climbed into the vehicle.

"I'm glad we could help."

From the passenger seat, Dierdre enthusiastically rubbed her hands together. "Time to play detective."

Harriet couldn't summon a smile in response to her intern's zeal. As much as she wanted to find Prince Charming for the Danbys' sake, she didn't relish the prospect of finding him at their neighbor's. "This needs to be a friendly visit, okay? We'll poke around if we can, but we shouldn't say anything that suggests we're suspicious of him. Agreed?"

"You're the boss."

Somehow Dierdre's happy-go-lucky response didn't reassure Harriet.

They found Mr. Wilcox in his workshop, painting a photo-shoot prop of a shepherdess and her lamb. Harriet, who'd previously met her wiry, balding neighbor at a community event, introduced Dierdre.

"What brings you here?" he asked, sounding suspicious. Or maybe it was Dierdre's suspicions of him that made his response to their arrival seem that way.

"I thought I'd make some complimentary calls to neighboring farms, given the recent disappearance of the Danbys' prizewinning ram. Did you hear about that?"

"Aye." He resumed painting curly blond hair around the hole where eager children would pose with toothy smiles. "They called to ask if I'd seen it."

"I'm concerned that a loose dog might have been worrying the sheep. Did you notice a dog running around your farm Sunday night?"

"Nope." The man's stern gaze shifted from Harriet to Dierdre. "I like dogs as much as the next fellow. Every sheep farmer worth his salt knows the value of a decent sheepdog. But dog owners have to take responsibility for their animals."

"Of course." Harriet sidestepped him for a glimpse of the small pasture behind his barn. It was inaccessible from the road or the public path along the cliff, making it the ideal spot to hide a kidnapped ram. "I'd be happy to assess your flock for any signs of stress that might indicate they've encountered a rogue dog. At no charge of course."

"No thanks." He focused on cleaning his paintbrush. "If a sheep farmer can't tell that for himself, he should get out of the business."

"I'd hoped to gain a clearer picture of whether we're dealing with a wider problem, or if the missing animal merely wandered off."

"Or was nicked," Dierdre interjected.

Harriet shot her a glare, scrambling to think of a lighthearted quip to convince her neighbor they weren't there to accuse *him* of stealing Prince Charming.

Mr. Wilcox's eyes narrowed at Dierdre's suggestion. "Is that what Danby thinks? Sheep rustling has become a huge problem in this country. You've got organized gangs driving tractor-trailers that make off with a whole flock in one night."

"In the UK?" Harriet's voice squeaked in surprise. She'd heard of instances of large-scale rustling like that in the US, but she didn't know it happened here.

"Aye. Thankfully on a main road like this, they'd have a hard time getting away with a stunt like that." Mr. Wilcox added a touch of black to the nose of his lamb image. "The worst is when farmers target other farmers. No one wants to grass on their neighbor."

"Grass on?" Harriet repeated.

"Report," Dierdre translated.

"I see." Harriet couldn't help but wonder if the comment was his backhanded way of chastising them, or his way of giving the impression his hands were as clean as the painted lamb's pure white fleece.

Mr. Wilcox touched up the lamb's hoofs. "Makes for bad blood if you're wrong. But there was a case a few years ago of a farmer who set up a dodgy abattoir at his place. He had stolen beasts brought in for butchering and sold the meat under the table."

"That is concerning." Meat safety rules were established for a reason. Those thieves would have no idea what medicine might still be in the system of a stolen animal, let alone whether it had a disease that made it unfit for consumption.

"The reality is," Mr. Wilcox continued, cleaning his paintbrush once more, "that when farmers graze their sheep on common land, they're bound to lose a few head every so often. It's nigh impossible to know for sure whether the beasts wandered off, were attacked, or got nicked."

"That's true," Dierdre agreed. "My brother said that because farmers aren't sure, they often don't report missing sheep."

"So the police might not be aware how widespread a sheep-rustling problem could be?" Harriet asked. She'd have to start asking clients about their losses to see if she could detect a pattern. If the losses were as common as Mr. Wilcox suggested, maybe Dusty was innocent after all. And maybe she wasn't to blame for the other missing ewes either.

Dierdre elbowed Harriet and tilted her head toward the side of the barn. "I'll keep him busy, you look for the tup," she said under her breath. Then she raised her voice and said, "These props are brilliant. Did you draw them yourself?"

Mr. Wilcox's leathery cheeks creased into his first smile since they'd arrived. "My youngest daughter did. She's studying art in school."

Dierdre flexed her question-asking prowess while Harriet slipped around to the rear of the barn.

The small fold enclosed ten ewes, all of which were likely due to give birth within the week. There wasn't a ram in sight.

A loud bleating sounded from inside the barn.

Harriet hurried to the closest dust-caked window and cupped her hands to peer in. She managed to make out a ram hanging its head over the stall wall.

"Hey. What are you doing?" Mr. Wilcox demanded from behind, making her jump.

CHAPTER SIX

Her heart thumping, Harriet faced Mr. Wilcox, knowing the way she'd jumped at his question made her look guilty. "Someone doesn't sound happy in there." She hitched her thumb at the barn window. "I guess it's instinct for me to see what the problem is."

"There's nothing wrong with the beast."

Dierdre rounded the corner of the barn and mouthed, "Sorry."

Mr. Wilcox swiped red paint off his hand with the rag dangling from his jeans pocket. "He'll be happy enough when he's on his new patch." He waved off further questions. "I don't have time for any more chitchat. We're opening at the end of the week, and I still have props to prepare. And lambs due soon."

"I noticed that," Harriet said. "If any of your ewes run into trouble, don't hesitate to call." She handed him a business card then tugged Dierdre toward the Beast.

Inside the vehicle, Harriet told Dierdre what she'd seen. Dierdre stared at Mr. Wilcox through the front windshield. "I don't trust him. Guaranteed that tup will be gone before he opens his farm to the public at the end of the week."

"You could be right, but barring sudden trouble with a lambing, I'm not sure how we can sneak a peek in there before then," Harriet said.

"Polly said you're stepping out with the pastor, right?"

Ignoring the heat rising to her cheeks, Harriet focused on starting the Beast. "Yes. How does that help?"

"Do the Wilcoxes go to your church?"

"No."

Dierdre frowned as they started back toward the clinic. "Too bad. He could've paid a pastoral visit. Maybe I could ask my brother to stop in to ask Mr. Wilcox if he wants to add sheepdog herding demos to his events schedule."

"Hey, that could work. Do you think he'd do it?"

"If there's a chance of a job in it for him, he'll be here quicker than you can say, 'hire me.'"

"It's probably better if Mr. Wilcox doesn't know Tristan is your brother. That way his turning up uninvited doesn't arouse any suspicions."

"No problem. But how is Tristan supposed to know if the tup belongs to the Danbys? I know he's a champion, but they kind of all look the same to the untrained eye. And Mr. Wilcox would be onto him in a flash if Tristan got caught looking at the ear tag."

"Actually, Prince Charming has a distinctive freckle in his right ear, plus a habit of winking at you when you look into his eyes. Hence his name."

"Will he wink at anyone, or just pretty vets?" Dierdre teased.

Harriet chuckled. "He does it to the Danby kids. They named him."

"All right then. I'll let you know what Tristan finds out."

After Dierdre went home to cajole her brother into spying for them, Harriet headed to the library to sift through their historical documents, hoping it would take her mind off what she'd need to tell Dusty's owners if the ram in Mr. Wilcox's barn wasn't Prince Charming. It wouldn't prove that Dusty was to blame for Prince Charming's going missing. Sheep rustlers were still a possibility. But given the timing of Dusty's escape, he was the more likely culprit.

On the drive to the library, Harriet called Will to update him on the newest development.

"I hope you're wrong about Mr. Wilcox being involved," Will told her. "I don't know the man personally, but if you can't trust your neighbors, life is much less pleasant."

"I know, but I want the ram found for Doreen's sake."

Will's tone softened. "You do know the Danbys will forgive you if Dusty is to blame for the disappearance, don't you? You couldn't have known he'd dig a hole under the fence when he's never tried to before."

"I know they will. They're wonderful people. And I'll make restitution, though Prince Charming was a champion. He won't be easy to replace." She sighed at the other thought that had been bothering her—that her culpability in the matter, not to mention the other missing ewes, would tarnish her reputation with area farmers.

"I'm still praying he'll turn up," Will said, as if he could read her mind. "In the meantime, don't borrow trouble."

"Easier said than done."

"If I didn't have a counseling session tonight, I'd take you to tea."

Harriet's heart warmed. "I'll take a rain check on that offer."

"If you're able to make tomorrow night's Bible study at church, perhaps we could go afterward?"

"I'd like that."

"I'm glad. Have a good evening," he said, sounding reluctant to hang up.

"You too, Will." Harriet touched her earbud, disconnecting the call, and parked outside the converted stone cottage that served as the village's library. She grabbed her notebook and pen then froze with her hand on the door handle.

Simon Boyes flashed a wad of cash to the guy walking beside him on the sidewalk in front of her. Will had said that Simon arrived in town broke and unemployed. How did he have so much money?

Harriet watched the pair head toward the lower bay. Should she ask Will to confront Simon about the apparent windfall? As big a leap in logic as it might be, his becoming flush within days of Prince Charming's disappearance was way too coincidental for comfort.

On the other hand, if Simon had come by the money honestly, he'd lose any respect he might have for Will if Will misjudged him and jumped to the wrong conclusion. But if Simon had gotten the money from selling the Danbys' ram, and they demanded he tell them who he sold it to, there might still be time to get Prince Charming back.

She tried calling Will, but the call went to voice mail. He must be busy in his counseling session. She stared after Simon, wondering if she should follow him. Being broke gave him motive. And Will said he worked as a farm laborer, which gave him opportunity.

Before Harriet could decide, the pair disappeared with the dip of the road as an elderly couple emerged from a nearby yard.

Realizing how strange it would look if she went tearing after a couple of young men, Harriet nixed the impulse to confront Simon and opted to stick to her original research plans for the evening. It was just as likely that he'd gotten a job helping a local farm during their busy lambing season. She had no evidence that he'd made money through unsavory means, and nothing but hearsay as a reason to suspect him in the first place.

Harriet introduced herself to the librarian and was soon set up with the microfiche machine in the library's basement. In no time at all she found herself immersed in the postwar era of the late 1940s. The decline of tenant farming. The replacement of horses with tractors. The revolutionary introduction of antimicrobials into veterinary care. All while the government debt soared to 270 percent of the GDP. Thankfully, loans from the US kept the economy functioning. But even bread, which had never been rationed during the war, was brought under government control.

The sheep-burying blizzard of February 1947 must have felt like the final death blow to many Yorkshire farmers. Harriet skimmed microfiche copies of several Yorkshire newspapers from the weeks following the blizzard. Most of the local news amounted to social gossip about the comings and goings of landowners. Harriet supposed the landed gentry were the closest thing to celebrities of their day.

Then, in a column dated six weeks after the blizzard, she read:

No one has seen or heard from Kingsbury Estate tenant farmer Samuel Bishop in weeks, and neighbors fear the worst, even as theories regarding his disappearance abound.

Like many North Yorkshire sheep farmers, Bishop lost his entire flock to the blizzard. Many believe Bishop succumbed to a broken heart while wandering the moors. But others insist his involvement in a clandestine government project got him killed. The government declined to comment

*on the rumor that Bishop's animals were secreted away under
the cover of darkness.*

The police are investigating.

Harriet straightened in her chair. "Now we're getting somewhere. I wonder if I could get my hands on those police reports. I'll
have to stop by the department to see."

"Dr. Bailey?" The librarian trotted down the stairs and across
the room to Harriet. "I'm afraid it's past closing time."

"I'm sorry. I completely lost track of time. I didn't mean to keep
you." Harriet removed the microfiche from the machine.

"Not a problem." The curly-haired young man in wire-rimmed
glasses returned the film to the correct file. "I'm staying for the historical society's meeting down here anyway."

"You're a history buff?"

"I am."

"Then perhaps you can help me. Are you familiar with the story
of Samuel Bishop and his dog?"

The young man chuckled. "The ghost dog? That's been a favorite tale for generations."

"Most farmers keep breeding records or journals or such. You
wouldn't happen to know where I might find any of Samuel Bishop's
that might have survived, would you?"

"Bishop's place was a tenant farm on the Kingsbury Estate. You
might try there. You could also try the livestock auction. They keep
records of every animal that goes through the place, cataloged by farm.
You should be able to find a list of everything he bought or sold."

"As far back as 1947?"

"From the day they opened in 1926, I believe. They recently contacted the historical society to ask if we'd be interested in keeping the records after their centennial celebration next year."

"That's perfect. Thank you." Perhaps Harriet didn't have answers yet, but at least she had some promising steps to try.

The next day was Wednesday—auction day. As luck would have it, Harriet had a farm call less than a mile from the livestock auction. At the sight of the parking lot full of farm vehicles, she realized that auction day was probably not the best day to inquire about viewing old records, but since she was already there, she might as well.

Spotting Dr. Nigel Ellerby exiting his vehicle, Harriet strode over to him. "Are you the sale barn vet?" Nigel was one of what she called the Old Boys Club—some of her grandad's colleagues, who'd kindly welcomed her when she took over his practice.

"Just for today," he replied. "Their regular vet had a family emergency, and someone has to see that the buyers get what they pay for."

"True enough." Harriet told him to have a good day and headed to the cramped, dusty office.

The petite, white-haired woman behind the desk hung up the phone and reclipped her earring to her ear. "May I help you?"

Harriet introduced herself and explained what she hoped to find.

"How wonderful." The woman smacked her hands together with a gleeful grin and sprang from her chair. "That is exactly the kind of research I'd hoped the records might inspire. I even sent feelers to all the country's agricultural colleges. I got the idea after a lad came in to compile a breed history for a farm he was looking to partner in." The woman led Harriet to a large storage room filled from floor to ceiling with file boxes.

Thankfully the boxes were labeled by year. Harriet selected three from 1946, the year before Samuel died. In the third box, she found a file for Samuel Bishop, but he'd only sold at auction, not purchased.

She checked the boxes for the two years prior and found records of his purchases of several different breeds, both rams and ewes. She opened the note app on her phone and recorded the information. But even as she did, she feared she was grasping at straws by trying to make more of Samuel Bishop's history than she could possibly prove.

Maybe Polly was right. Rowena's husband might not be willing to admit he was a secret agent, but he might be willing to help her find out whether the government had ever run a secret sheep-breeding program. Then again, wouldn't something like that have been in the agricultural department's realm? Why would it have needed to be a secret?

Hearing the beginning of the auction, Harriet quickly reshelved the boxes. She still had another farm call to make before returning to the clinic.

She stepped outside and studied the list of the day's sellers tacked to the board outside the ring. At the sight of a ram from Wilcox's Wanderings on the list, her pulse jumped.

Dierdre had texted last night that Tristan had paid Mr. Wilcox a visit with no more success at getting a peek inside the man's barn than they'd had. But Mr. Wilcox couldn't keep Harriet from seeing the ram here. She scanned the faces around the ring but couldn't see Mr. Wilcox. Spotting Nigel, she hurried over to him. "Where's Wilcox's ram?"

"It was the first sale of the day."

"Where is it now?"

"Buyer drove around to the chute and picked him up already."

"Do you know who bought it?"

"No. Why?"

Harriet bit her lip. "I think it might've been the Danbys' stolen ram."

Nigel eyed her, his craggy features stern. "That's a mighty serious accusation. You'd better be positive before you cast aspersions like that."

"I know, and I'm not positive. I'm trying to find out. Did you record the number on the ear tag?"

"Of course." He thumbed through the paperwork on the clipboard he held. "The transponder in the EID tag didn't work, but the pastern band was intact." The two tags were supposed to contain the same information, which included the flock mark of the holding where the animal had been tagged, as well as its official identification number. "Here it is." Nigel showed it to Harriet. "It seems to be in order. Although now that I think about it, the flock mark was oddly worn. I had to guess at a couple of the numbers, but they must have matched Wilcox's Wanderings."

Harriet nodded, seeing in Nigel's examination notes that the ram was the same age and breed as Prince Charming. "Did he have a freckle in his ear?"

"Can't say I noticed."

"Did he wink at you when you examined his eyes?"

Nigel laughed. "The fabled winking tup. I've heard tales about that beast. You're saying the tales are true?"

"They are."

"Well, the one I examined didn't wink at me."

Harriet deflated. It was possible Prince Charming simply hadn't felt like winking after his hectic few days. Or this ram wasn't him. "Okay. Thanks." She ducked back into the office to ask about the buyer, thinking she could pay him a friendly visit, but the receptionist was gone.

Harriet's phone alarm beeped the half-hour alert she'd set so she'd have time to check on the Fairburns' pony before morning clinic hours. The drive alone would practically take her most of that, so following up on the sale would have to wait.

When she reached the Fairburn farm, a police cruiser sat in the driveway.

Her pulse jumped. *Get a grip. There are a million reasons why the police might be here.* But the Fairburns did have several valuable flocks of sheep. Mrs. Fairburn had just been telling Dierdre yesterday about the Border Leicesters they were breeding, a rarity these days, not to mention their prizewinning Texel-Swaledale crosses.

Stock of either breed would fetch more at auction than Prince Charming. And with the possibility that he'd been sold at today's auction on her mind, it was no wonder her first thought at the sight of the police car was, *Did sheep rustlers strike again?*

CHAPTER SEVEN

Harriet could make out the silhouette of a uniformed officer standing inside the door of the Fairburns' house, so she took her time gathering her veterinary bag as the impulse to know what was going on warred with the responsibility to mind her own business.

When she'd seen the pony yesterday afternoon, Tanya had greeted her, but she'd be in school this morning. Harriet shuffled her feet. Would Mrs. Fairburn expect her to call at the house before going to the barn?

When Harriet reached the point where she either needed to choose the path to the front door or the other to the barn, Detective Constable Van Worthington stepped out of the house.

Harriet lifted a hand in silent greeting, and Van headed toward her. His pained expression made her suspect that Polly, not whatever Mrs. Fairburn had called to report, was on his mind.

When he reached her, Van asked, "How's Polly?" The glimmer of hope in his eyes said he wasn't ready to abandon his dream of a happily-ever-after with the woman. He clearly still loved her despite the hurt.

Harriet offered him a sympathetic smile. "She seems about as miserable as you are, if I'm being honest. I think the two of you need a little time to sort out your feelings."

He cleared his throat. "Yeah, maybe so."

"I know you both care for each other. I'm sure it'll work out the way it's supposed to."

He took a deep breath and squared his shoulders. "Thank you, Harriet."

"You're welcome." Harriet prayed she hadn't given him false hope. But she truly believed Polly and Van were meant to be. She glanced at the house, a little surprised that Mrs. Fairburn hadn't come out yet to see her to the pony. "What's happened here?"

"They had a couple gimmers go missing from the south field. Mrs. Fairburn thinks they were stolen." His tone was skeptical.

Harriet gasped. "This is the third incident in less than a week."

"What are you talking about?" Van whipped his notepad and pen from his pocket. "This is the first I've heard of any other missing livestock."

Harriet's pulse quickened as a clearer picture of what had been happening solidified in her mind. Maybe none of the disappearances had been her fault. "The Huckabys lost three ewes Saturday. The Danbys discovered their ram missing Monday. And almost two weeks ago now, the Trussels had a newly purchased ram go missing. I don't think any of them seriously thought the stock might've been stolen, which is probably why they didn't report the disappearances. But with the Fairburns losing some ewes, it sure seems as if we've got a sheep rustler in our midst."

Van's eyes widened. "Do you know if the other farmers saw anyone nosing around their places beforehand?"

"Not that they mentioned."

Van hitched his thumb to the farmhouse. "The Fairburns didn't either."

Harriet's thoughts veered to yesterday afternoon's drive. Dierdre's brother had been out with his dog in a field south of the farm. But she'd met Tristan. He was a nice guy. His reason for being there was probably entirely innocent. "Do the Fairburns know when it happened?"

"They assume last night because they saw truck lights out that way shortly after eleven. But by the time Mr. Fairburn got himself dressed and outside, they'd left. Then, sure enough, this morning's head count came up short."

Harriet nodded, not sure if the time frame left Tristan out of the picture or not.

"Of course, Mr. Fairburn hadn't done a head count since Sunday morning, so they could've gone missing earlier. Maybe the same day as Danbys' ram. I'll speak to Tom." Van closed his notepad and shoved it into his pocket. "I told Mrs. Fairburn I'd alert the livestock auction to be on the lookout for the gimmers. Might get lucky and have someone try to sell them who's not smart enough to change the ear tags."

"I just came from there, and I think Mr. Wilcox might have sold the Danbys' ram." Harriet bit her lip, instantly regretting that she'd said the words out loud.

"Wilcox? Your neighbor?"

Harriet squirmed. "I thought he might begrudge the Danbys competing with him for half-term tourists. Then when I was at his place yesterday, he acted kind of cagey. Didn't want me to see a ram he had in the barn."

"You showed up at his place uninvited?" Van shook his head.

"Yes. But the point is, if the sheep was his, why would he care if I saw it? It made me think he was afraid I'd recognize it as the Danbys'."

Van made more notes, his lips pressed into a thin line. "Okay, I'll talk to him."

"Actually, maybe don't do that yet. But if you're going to the livestock auction, could you find out who bought the ram he sold?"

"Aye. I'll call the Danbys for their missing tup's ear-tag number then pay a visit to the buyer and see if the numbers match."

"I'd be happy to visit the buyer's farm for you if you get the address. I know how busy you are."

Van hesitated. Finally, he said in a stern tone, "Okay, but if you discover it's the Danbys', you leave it for me to deal with."

"You got it." Harriet motioned to the barn. "I'd better see to my patient."

Once inside the barn, she realized she'd forgotten to ask Van whether he could help her access the police department's archives. Making a mental note to ask when he got in touch with her about the auction info, Harriet turned her full attention to examining the pony.

Thankfully, she seemed to be doing much better, and her hoof was no longer hot. As much as Harriet would have liked to stay and question Mrs. Fairburn about the sheep theft, she was already late for an appointment at the clinic.

The next few hours became a race to catch up.

That afternoon, Polly handed Harriet a mug of hot tea as she returned to the waiting room to collect her next patient. "Take a break and get yourself something to eat. Your next appointment for the day isn't for half an hour, and it's your last one."

"Fabulous. Thanks." Harriet slipped through the door to her kitchen and heated a can of soup. She needed to set aside time each week to cook a few meals ahead and make a big pot of homemade soup.

But emergency calls inevitably sabotaged her best intentions. She couldn't imagine keeping up this pace with a family. Yet somehow her grandfather had managed *and* found time to paint too. Of course, he'd had her grandmother to keep the home fires burning and hadn't started painting until later in his life, after his children had moved out.

Harriet sighed. *It must be the short, gray days getting to me.* Or the nagging fear that she'd let her imagination fabricate a sheep rustler trolling their community because it was easier to stomach than believing her inattention was to blame for the rash of missing sheep. Except Van had seemed to agree there was something to her theory.

Sitting at the table with her soup, she glanced at the calendar on the fridge, and her gut tightened. Friday was Valentine's Day, and Will had asked her to do her best to keep the date open so they could spend the evening together. Was that what had her insides in a knot?

This time last year, she'd been living and working in Connecticut, still smarting a little over her broken engagement. Now she was well and truly over Dustin, but maybe it was still too soon to get serious with someone new.

She shook her head and took another bite of soup. She loved spending time with Will. But Valentine's Day put ridiculous pressure on couples. Like the all-important card. Did she go for humorous? Or mushy romantic? Or something casual?

The thought of standing in the shop in front of all the card options was overwhelming.

Polly rushed into the kitchen. "Van's here." She cast about the room as if looking for a place to hide. "I, uh, need to go to the kennels and check on Dusty. His owners will be here soon to pick him up. Can you see what Van wants?"

Harriet lowered her spoon. "You can't avoid him forever."

"I won't. But I need to today." She motioned to the patio door. "I'll go out this way."

The office phone rang.

"Sorry," Harriet said. "I can't see what the detective constable wants and answer the phone too."

Polly threw up her hands. "Fine." She stomped toward the reception area.

Harriet quickly finished her soup before following Polly.

Van stood near the door, hat in hand, nervously kneading the brim. Polly was on the phone at her desk, facing away from him. At his doleful expression, Harriet's heart went out to him.

She rounded the reception desk to take Van's focus off of Polly. "You have news for me about who bought the ram at auction?" News he could have merely texted her, but then he wouldn't have had an excuse to see Polly.

"Aye." With obvious reluctance, Van shifted his gaze to Harriet. "A fellow by the name of Anderson bought it." He handed Harriet a slip of paper with an address.

From the corner of her eye, Harriet noticed that the mention of the Danbys' ram halted Polly's stealthy retreat after the phone call.

Dierdre strode in through the main door. "What's going on? Did you find Prince Charming?"

Van's face flamed an even darker shade of red. The poor man hadn't been told the missing sheep's name, so Harriet could imagine what he was thinking.

"We're not sure." Harriet filled her in on the auction-sale news.

"A lad in the sale barn said the auction house sent a truck to pick up Wilcox's tup this morning," Van added. "He said Wilcox didn't have a way to get the animal there because he blew the engine in his lorry. It's been in the shop since Friday."

"That was before Prince Charming disappeared." Dierdre frowned. "So he couldn't have stolen the tup."

"Sure he could have," Polly said. "He lives close enough to have walked it home, and if anyone asked him what he was up to, he could've said he found the tup wandering and was securing him until he found out who he belonged to."

"That's true," Dierdre agreed. "Our going there yesterday must've spooked him into wanting to offload it fast."

"Not necessarily," Harriet cautioned. "The ram was in the barn when we got there, presumably because Wilcox had already arranged to have it taken to auction."

Van cleared his throat. "And we don't know yet if it belongs to the Danbys."

"But it's looking more and more like theirs was stolen," Harriet added to Dierdre. "Do you remember the Fairburns, whose pony we examined yesterday afternoon? They've had two gimmers go missing."

Dierdre's eyes widened.

Was she thinking of her brother's unexpected presence in the area too? Harriet itched to ask, maybe phrase her question to suggest that he might have seen something. But she didn't want to bring up Tristan's presence near the Fairburn farm in front of Van before she knew anything for sure. She hadn't noticed a vehicle in the area when they drove by Tristan. And he would have needed one to spirit away a couple of sheep. Did he even own a vehicle?

"Before you go, Van," Harriet said when he returned his note-pad to his pocket, "I'm researching the Samuel Bishop story for a magazine article I'm working on. I read in the library's newspaper archives that the police investigated his disappearance. Do you know if your department would still have the report, and if so, how I'd go about requesting access?"

"Reports are kept until the subject is a hundred years old, but they're not public. Not unless they've been revealed in court."

"This report would've been generated in 1947," Harriet said. "Could you ask someone if I might be able to have access if it's still on file?"

"I'll see what I can do, but no promises," Van told her. "Oh, there is something else that could be pertinent to the thefts. The Whitby police found the delivery van that belongs to Galloway's General Store abandoned by an empty warehouse on the edge of town."

"Do you think the sheep rustlers nicked it?" Polly asked, her face flashing red when the question drew Van's attention back to her.

"I do. The officer who called in the report said there was evidence that animals had been transported in it. And the timing fits."

"When was the van stolen?" Harriet asked.

"The Galloways aren't sure. It was their old one, and they'd lent it to a friend a while ago. But their friends are away this week. Gavin figures it must've been taken some time after this past Saturday morning, which is when their friends left."

"I saw a large vehicle speed off from the end of my driveway Sunday night around six," Harriet said. "I'm not sure if it had been up by the house or was merely turning around at the end of the drive. But it headed north."

Van added the information to his notes. "Thanks for telling me. If not for the livestock thefts, we would probably attribute it to some teens taking it for a joyride."

Harriet's thoughts veered to the giddy group of lads she and Will had run into. The one boy had let slip that they'd been in Whitby, and even Simon had hinted as much when he recommended the Whitby Abbey ruins. Should she mention seeing him with a wad of cash last night, though he was supposed to be broke?

"Simon Boyes is back in town." Polly sliced the briefest glance in Van's direction. "He stole a car a few years ago, remember?"

"I plan to talk to him."

"You might want to ask him if he's been working," Harriet suggested, taking advantage of the opening Polly had given her. "I spotted him in town last night with a surprising amount of money in hand. It caught my attention because Will mentioned that Simon had returned to town flat broke."

Van jotted the information into his notepad.

Harriet hoped Will wouldn't be cross with her for sharing that with the detective constable. She hadn't perceived that he'd shared it in confidence and hoped he didn't see it that way.

Because if Simon was stealing vans and livestock for quick cash, he needed to be brought to justice.

CHAPTER EIGHT

Happy as she was that Van was taking a keen interest in the livestock disappearances, Harriet nevertheless advised Polly to caution Dusty's owners when they picked him up. "Tell them that he dug his way out of his run and might have chased a few sheep, though we're not sure. So they should take appropriate precautions. Let them know what Mike did here."

"Will do."

Turning to Dierdre, Harriet said, "I don't have any farm calls scheduled for this afternoon, so unless an emergency comes in, we're done for the day. But you're welcome to come along with me to the Andersons to see the ram they bought at auction."

"Seeing different farms is always an education," Dierdre said eagerly.

Later, as they drove the winding, hilly rural roads, Dierdre asked, "So, have you made any progress on your research for the magazine article?"

"Not yet. The librarian suggested I pay the Kingsbury Estate a visit, since Samuel was one of their tenant farmers."

"Reggie lives near there."

"I'm not sure how they'd feel about my showing up unannounced, but if you're game, we could try stopping in there after we visit the Anderson farm."

"Sure thing."

The Anderson farm boasted a modern home and barns beside pastures with a variety of sheep breeds, including valuable rare breeds like Babydolls and Valais Blacknose sheep.

"It seems Mr. Anderson is going after the niche market," Harriet observed.

"Reggie says farmers with limited pastureland can only make a go at full-time farming if they specialize."

"It sounds like Reggie knows his business."

Dierdre beamed. "He's super smart. He studied computer science and business at university. But when his grandfather offered him a chance to take over the family farm, he couldn't resist."

"Grandfathers are the best." Harriet winked at Dierdre, who was well aware that Harriet had inherited her veterinary practice and home from her own grandad.

"My grandparents are in their late sixties and still farming full-time. I can't imagine my grandfather ever retiring, but I think he's been talking to my dad and uncle about succession plans. My dad says we should plant more trees to sell carbon credits to big business."

"It's kind of sad that that's more profitable to do than farm."

"Aye. Tristan shepherds for our grandfather and does contract milking at another farm. But neither pays that great, so he tries to pick up whatever other work he can."

"Sounds as if he has a terrific work ethic." Harriet's heart pounded. She might never have a better segue to ask about Tristan without sounding suspicious of him. She cleared her throat. "Did you happen to ask your brother what he was doing by the Fairburns' place yesterday afternoon?"

"No, I never did."

"I didn't want to mention seeing him to the detective constable before talking to you, because I don't want him to think I suspect your brother."

Dierdre stared at her, eyes wide.

"I don't," Harriet quickly added. "But he might've seen something he doesn't realize could be a clue."

"I never thought of that. I'll ask him tonight."

When she spotted the sign for the Andersons' farm, Harriet turned into the driveway.

A rotund man in denim overalls approached when she stepped out of the vehicle. "You Doc Bailey's granddaughter?"

"That's right." She tilted her head. "Have we met?"

"No. I recognize the dent in your vehicle's front fender. My bull put it there when your grandfather drove into the wrong field to see to a sick cow." The man chuckled, his amusement carving deep laugh lines in his cheeks and around his eyes.

Harriet smiled. "I think I remember hearing that story."

The man offered his hand to shake. "Name's Bob Anderson. What brings you here?"

Harriet shook his hand and introduced Dierdre. "We'd like to double-check the ID on the ram you bought at auction today. Some of the numbers were difficult for the duty vet to read. Were you informed the transponder on the EID tag didn't work?"

"Aye. I'll see to getting it replaced." Mr. Anderson motioned to the barn. "The tup is in here if you want to see him. I always worm and quarantine new stock before releasing them into the pasture, so he shouldn't be difficult to catch."

"Great. Lead the way."

Once inside the barn, Mr. Anderson filled a feed bucket with pellets then let himself into the pen and rattled the bucket.

The ram eyed Harriet suspiciously, which was her first clue she wasn't looking at Prince Charming. The Danbys' ram was so tame, he wouldn't have hesitated to go for the feed bucket.

Mr. Anderson held the ram by the fleece, and Harriet checked his ear tag, or rather, his ear. No telltale freckle. Harriet noted the tag number in her phone's note app anyway and tamped down her disappointment. She should be happy this cleared Mr. Wilcox of sheep rustling. The bad blood between neighbors would have been horrible.

In fact, she was beginning to feel mortified that she'd so easily convinced herself Mr. Wilcox could be guilty simply because he'd been standoffish. But had he been, really? She'd assumed all his talk about sheep rustling was his way of deflecting her questions. That had probably been wishful thinking on her part, with her desire to clear Dusty from responsibility.

As they walked back to the truck, Harriet texted Van that she'd been wrong about Mr. Wilcox while Dierdre quizzed Mr. Anderson about his flock and his plans for the new addition. Pride lit the man's face as he raved about his livestock—the size of the lambs last year and not a single loss at birth.

Opening the Beast's door, Harriet thanked him for his time.

"I wish I'd known you were coming. I have a handful of cows that are due for their TB testing." The man scratched his whiskery chin. "I don't suppose you have what you need with you to do that now?"

"I don't. I'm sorry. But if you call the office, Polly would be happy to get that scheduled for you."

"I'll do that."

"Do you see many cases of TB these days?" Dierdre asked as they climbed into the Land Rover.

"Not in this area, thankfully." Harriet shifted the Beast into gear. "It's already four o'clock. Do you still want to go to the Kingsbury Estate with me?"

"Absolutely."

"Great. Do you know how to get us there from here?"

"One second." Dierdre switched on her phone and opened the map app. She relayed directions that took them up and down steep hills in the heart of the moors, until… "Brilliant. I lost my signal."

"You said the estate was near where your boyfriend lives. Do you recognize any of the landmarks around here?"

Dierdre peered out the window. "I'm not sure."

Harriet slowed as they approached an intersection and read the street name aloud. "Ring any bells?"

"Right. Kingsbury's road forks off that one."

"Perfect." Harriet soon found the sprawling estate. "Wow. Is this guy a lord or something?"

"He's a baron, I think."

She groaned. "What are the chances I can show up on his doorstep and convince him to speak to me? The butler will take one look at the Beast and tell me to come around to the trade entrance."

"He's not who you'll want to talk to anyway. The farm manager will know more about the history of the tenant farms and their stewards than the lord of the manor."

"Good point."

Minutes later, they were ensconced in the farm manager's office, a large room lined with bookcases filled with journals. Harriet explained to the kind elderly man what background information she hoped to glean from Samuel Bishop's records, if they had them.

The man gave her a peculiar look, perhaps surprised that an American vet was interested in their estate's breeding history. Nevertheless, he soon located several pertinent journals. "These might have what you're after. You're welcome to look through them here, but I'm afraid I can't allow you to take them with you."

"This place is amazing," Dierdre whispered when the man left to see to other obligations.

Since Samuel died in early 1947, Harriet started with a journal dated 1945, while Dierdre scanned one from the previous year.

Moors near White Church Bay
August 2, 1945

When a strange lorry stopped on the lane, Samuel called instructions to his sheepdog. Shep instantly swept the field from side to side, herding the sheep away from the dodgy-looking bloke who climbed out of the lorry and peered over the hedgerow.

Samuel's skin crawled. The war in Europe might be over, but with food still scarce, the black market continued to thrive. And he'd heard that farmers who didn't "agree" to contribute might find themselves short a head or two with nothing put in their pocket to show for it.

"Come by," Samuel called to the dog. Then he said to the stranger, "Nothing to see here."

The man scraped his hand over his beard and lingered as the dog herded the sheep Samuel's way. "Nice sheep you've got."

Not trusting the stranger but not wanting to be rude either, Samuel touched the brim of his hat to acknowledge the compliment.

"How much for one of the lambs?" the man bellowed in a deep voice that easily carried across the heath.

"They're not for sale."

"Everything has a price."

"Walk on," Samuel called to his dog, turning his back on the man. He hadn't sunk to participating in the black market through the entire war. He wasn't about to start now.

When Samuel returned to the house for his evening tea, the man was waiting for him, sitting on the porch as if he were the lord of the manor himself. Samuel stalked toward him. "I already told you. The sheep are not for sale."

"That's why I'm here."

Samuel bristled. "You won't change my mind."

"I don't want to." The man flashed an official badge. "We'd like to collaborate with you."

Samuel narrowed his eyes. "Is that your fancy way of talking about sales under the table?"

"Not at all. Word around the moors is that you're an honest sort—a fact you've already proven to me—and that you're a top-notch breeder. Exactly the kind of man we want to work with."

"Who's 'we'?"

"Her Majesty's government. The Ministry of Food and Agriculture, to be exact. The country's supply chain is in crisis, and we need your help."

Samuel studied the man warily. "I already sell all my market lambs to the government."

"We've created a new program that we believe you'll agree is mutually beneficial."

Shep dropped at Samuel's feet and growled. Samuel silently agreed with his dog. I don't trust this bloke either. *He folded his arms over his chest.*

"I assure you we are in earnest. We want to commission you to establish a British super breed—meatier, faster growing, hardier, and with better feed conversion."

Samuel snorted. "Sheep farmers always make their breeding decisions with those goals in mind. At least the ones raising them for meat rather than wool."

"Yes. But you've been consistently successful at it." *The man took a step closer, as if satisfied Samuel was hooked and it was time to reel him in.* "Our program will help you raise the standard to a brand-new level in a fraction of the time it would take you without our assistance."

Samuel raised an eyebrow. "What's the catch?"

"No catch. But you must agree to keep meticulous records, and above all, tell no one about your work and our partnership agreement."

"Why would the government be so secretive about its programs to help people?"

"It's no different than development undertaken for the war effort, protected under the War Secrets Act. One never knows who might be a spy for foreign powers." *The man's gaze drifted to the manor house in the distant vale.* "I'm sure the baron frequently entertains foreign business interests."

Samuel's gaze widened. Was this man implying that Samuel's landlord knowingly entertained spies? Or was a spy himself?

Granted, Samuel had heard rumors that plenty of nobs sought out less-than-legal ways to supply food for their people, but that was a far cry from selling secrets to a foreign power.

Harriet mused over the journal entry. Maybe there *was* something to the rumor that the government had made Samuel disappear.

CHAPTER NINE

Stunned by what she'd read, Harriet blew out a breath. "I think I've found confirmation that the government commissioned Samuel to establish a new super breed of sheep." She showed Dierdre the journal entry then flipped through the remaining pages in search of actual breeding records. "I'm expecting Texels to figure into his breeding program, since they're known for their lean meat, twin births, and relatively low feed requirements. I'm sure I read that they were developed in the early part of the last century."

"But we didn't import them into the UK until the 1970s. My grandfather was actually one of the first farmers to breed them in these parts."

"Oh." Harriet stared at the list of lambs born on the Bishop farm in 1945. "I wonder if the government managed to get some into the country before that, but unofficially."

"Do you think that's possible?" Dierdre asked.

"I think we have to consider every option, even if it seems unlikely." Seeing nothing in the 1945 records to suggest that Samuel had changed his breeding tactics, Harriet moved on to the 1946 journal. "I can't make heads or tails of the notations in this book." She snapped pictures of several pages with her phone. "It's as if he started coding his records."

"So they couldn't be deciphered if they fell into the wrong hands?" Dierdre speculated.

"Could be. My aunt Jinny is a bit of a code aficionado. I'll see if she can make sense of this."

Dierdre leaned over and scanned the page Harriet had open. Pointing to a symbol, she said, "That kind of resembles a door. Maybe it stands for Dorset. They have an extended breeding season, so that would have made them valuable for continued meat supply."

"Except they're valued more for their wool than meat. It could also stand for Dorper. But I think Dorpers were still only in South Africa at that point." Harriet did a quick search on her phone and confirmed that the first Dorper lamb born in the UK was in 2005. Expelling a sigh, she photographed a few more cryptic journal pages for her aunt to examine. "As intriguing as Samuel's story is shaping up to be, using it for my article hook could become more work than it might be worth."

"Not necessarily. This squiggly line looks like an *S*, which probably stands for Suffolk. It's been the most popular sire breed in the UK for a long time because the lambs grow fast and have lots of muscle."

"That's true, but it could be Swaledale, especially if Samuel was striving for a hardy breed to withstand the harsher winters farther north."

"Or even Shropshire. They're hardy, but you see them more in the lowlands. Is there anything that looks like *HD*?" Dierdre scanned the new page. "The Hampshire Down have a good feed conversion rate and are hardy. My grandparents used to have a small flock."

The farm manager poked his head into the office. "Did you find what you were after?"

"Somewhat." Harriet stared at the strange code on the page in front of her. "Do you think there's any truth to the rumor that circulated in the late 1940s that Samuel Bishop disappeared because of a secret breeding project he was working on for the government?"

The man laughed heartily. "I dare say there's no one living on the estate today who would know either way, but if it'll bring more tourists, feel free to run with the story."

There was another angle for her story—that even apparently rich estates struggled to stay in the black.

Harriet asked him if he could help her interpret Samuel's code.

After perusing a few pages, he shook his head. "Has me stumped, lass. Sorry."

"That's okay." Ready to call it a day, Harriet closed the book. As the man walked them to her vehicle, she asked, "Have you or any of your tenant farmers had sheep go missing in recent weeks?"

"Not that I've heard. Why?"

"A few farms have, and the police are trying to discern whether they're isolated cases or something worse."

"Are they sure the sheep didn't simply wander off? The silly things do that occasionally."

"We're not sure of anything at this point." Harriet thanked him again, and they set off.

After dropping Dierdre at Cobble Hill to pick up her car and confirming that Dusty had been collected, Harriet drove into White Church Bay to pick up a few groceries and a Valentine's Day card for Will. As she entered Galloway's General Store, she waved to the owners, Gavin and Agnes, then headed straight for the card rack.

Like every other square inch of space in the shop, the card rack overflowed with stock of every size and style.

Zeroing in on the selection of Valentine's cards, Harriet read through half a dozen, growing increasingly uncomfortable. All were far too mushy for her current status with Will. She focused on the ones with animal pictures, hoping to find more common ground, since she was a vet and he seemed to love all animals. Reading the pithy lines, however, she quickly realized she wasn't sure how he'd take them.

Her first clue that Dustin wasn't the man for her should have been his first Valentine's Day card, which had read, *I like you almost as much as I like dogs*. As vets, they'd both thought it was hilarious, but in retrospect, she couldn't help wondering if he'd literally felt that way.

A woman next to her was looking at a card with a giant red heart on the front and *love* written in every font known to man all over it. "Harriet, isn't it?"

"That's right." Harriet smiled at the petite graying brunette. She recognized her but was having trouble pulling the name from her brain.

"I guess you're settling in nicely if you're already shopping for a Valentine's Day card," the woman teased. "Who's the lucky guy?"

"Mrs. Lindstrom," a deep male voice said from behind them, "I was hoping to catch you at Canterbury Travel before you closed for the day. Any chance you could spare me a few minutes once you're done with your shopping?"

The woman spun toward her would-be client. "Absolutely. Give me a second to pay for this, and I'll be right with you."

Clive Talbot winked at Harriet as Mrs. Lindstrom hurried to the counter. "You looked as if you could use rescuing."

"I guess you would know," she said, alluding to his fabled work as a secret agent.

His smirk confirmed that he understood her hint.

"How are Benji and Rowena doing?"

"Great."

"Aunt Jinny and I enjoyed the gorgeous gift basket you sent for Christmas. Thank you."

"The least we could do." His gaze shifted to the card rack, and he chose one to read.

Harriet refused to miss the opportunity. "I actually wanted to come and see you. I'm hoping you might help me with a bit of research I'm doing for a magazine article."

"Oh?" His voice held a strong undertone of hesitation.

"Are you familiar with the local legend about the shepherd and his ghost dog from the 1940s?"

Shaking his head, he traded the card in his hand for another. "Before my time, I'm afraid." Amusement laced his tone.

With a glance to confirm Mrs. Lindstrom was still waiting in line to pay for her card, Harriet gave Clive the highlights of the tale. "His journal suggests he might have accepted an offer to work on a secret government project. And I'm wondering where I might learn more about it, if that's possible."

"I don't doubt that the government commissioned such projects. The country was in a severe economic crisis following the Second World War. I'll ask around and see what I can dig up for you. No promises, you understand."

"I understand. Thank you for anything you can do," Harriet said.

Mrs. Lindstrom hurried toward them, teetering on her high heels. "Now, what can I help you with, Mr. Talbot?"

Clive returned the card he held to the rack and said goodbye to Harriet. "I've got an impromptu getaway to plan."

Harriet mirrored his wave and decided that having a former secret agent on her side had definite perks.

She opted for a card with two cartoon dogs sharing a picnic. It said, *Happy Valentine's Day* on the front but was blank inside. Hopefully she'd be able to think of something appropriate to write for Will by Friday.

CHAPTER TEN

When Harriet returned to the clinic, her steps faltered at the sight of the sparkly red hearts adorning the clinic's waiting room. Polly loved to decorate—from blue-and-white bunting for Yorkshire Day to sprigs of mistletoe and holly and brightly wrapped gifts galore for Christmas—but given her recent breakup, Harriet hadn't expected her to get into the spirit of this particular holiday.

Or was the sudden decorating spree Polly's attempt to convince herself she didn't still have feelings for Van?

Harriet left the Valentine's Day card she'd purchased for Will on her desk and headed to the kitchen to make dinner. Will had offered to take her to tea after the small group study, so she kept it light.

Leaving the dirty dishes in the sink to deal with later, she rushed upstairs to change and touch up her makeup. Not that she wore much, considering the hours she kept. But the circles under her eyes had grown darker than ever these past few days. And they'd only get worse when lambing and calving season got well underway.

She tied her hair up in a messy bun. Then, before heading to the Land Rover, she gave Maxwell and Charlie a few minutes of fuss, promising not to be late.

Aunt Jinny paused halfway to her own car. "You coming to small group?"

"I thought I'd give it a whirl since I have a free evening, barring an emergency call."

"That's great. We're starting a new series tonight. Your timing will seem perfectly natural."

Natural? Did Aunt Jinny think people would read something else into her joining the sessions? Harriet squirmed at the idea of people speculating on her motives. "On second thought, I should probably catch up on paperwork or work on my magazine article. In fact, I have some decoding I was hoping you could help me with from Samuel Bishop's journal. And I want to do a bit of research on sheep rustling to see if it sparks any ideas of where we might find Prince Charming." She'd just have to get another rain check on the tea from Will.

Aunt Jinny strode across the parking area and looped her arm through Harriet's. "Stop trying to talk yourself out of going."

"I'm not. It's just—"

"You were babbling. Your dad does the same thing when he's second-guessing a decision."

Harriet chuckled, familiar with that trait in her father. She'd never noticed the tendency in herself.

"You'll enjoy the evening. And I'd be happy to help you with decoding later," Aunt Jinny said.

Harriet nodded. "I better take the Beast in case I get an emergency call."

Aunt Jinny smirked. "Why do I get the feeling that scenario wouldn't bother you?"

Harriet bit her lip. "The truth is, I don't know if I'm ready for the questions that will inevitably follow my being seen more and more with Will. I don't know if people will approve of me for their pastor's wife."

"Pastor's wife?" Aunt Jinny's eyes widened. "Aren't you getting a little ahead of yourself?"

Harriet's face heated at her aunt's question. "Probably, but I need to consider these things early on in a relationship. I don't want to lose a year or two dating someone I don't have a future with."

"Are you thinking about having a family?"

"I've always thought I'd have a family one day." Her gaze drifted to her name on the sign at the clinic's entrance. "I can't imagine how I'd make it work now that I run my own clinic. I suppose I'd have to hire a second vet. But if I were married, I could afford a pay cut to keep the practice viable."

"Sounds like you've given this a lot of thought."

Harriet felt her cheeks blaze again, no doubt redder than the Valentine's Day hearts Polly had strewn about the waiting room. "Well, it seems important to consider, don't you think?"

"Maybe, but I don't think you'll do yourself or Will any favors by overthinking the relationship. If you ask me, there's been obvious attraction between the two of you from the start. You enjoy each other's company and share the same values. Stop putting so much pressure on yourself and ignore what other people think. If it's meant to be, it'll work out in God's perfect timing."

"You're right."

"And don't be afraid to talk to him about your thoughts."

Harriet balked at that prospect. "I couldn't do that. What would he think if I started questioning how we'd fit my practice and babies into our future together? Maybe he doesn't expect our relationship to progress beyond casual dating. It would totally freak him out."

"If that's the case, then wouldn't you want to know that sooner rather than later?"

"I suppose." Harriet's insides churned. "But I still think it's a little early to have that conversation."

Aunt Jinny's face crinkled into a smile. "How about for tonight you simply enjoy the fellowship and study?"

"Yes. We'd better get going, or we'll be late."

The church parking lot held about a quarter of the number of cars as it would on a Sunday morning. Will's wasn't among them, nor was it in the parsonage driveway next door.

Harriet walked to the parish hall entrance with Aunt Jinny. "Will leads these Wednesday night sessions, doesn't he?"

"Yes, why?"

"His car's not here."

"He was called to a hospital visit," a woman's voice chirped from behind them. They turned and greeted Elaine Dawson, Doreen Danby's older sister. "Pastor Will asked my Henry if he'd lead tonight's session."

"That's nice of Henry to stand in for him," Harriet said. "Is he already here?"

"He should be. He caught a ride in with our neighbor because I couldn't leave until my pies were done."

Harriet gave her a warm smile. Doreen and her sisters, Elaine and Maureen, were all gifted bakers.

The evening's study and resulting discussion were lively and engaging. Harriet thoroughly enjoyed the experience. At the end, Elaine asked that they pray for Prince Charming's safe return.

"Did Maureen's neighbor ever find his two ewes that went missing?" Mrs. Huddersley asked.

Harriet straightened in her seat. "What neighbor? When did this happen?"

"The Vail farm lost a couple ewes last November," Elaine explained. "They gathered all the sheep in for vaccinations, and the numbers came up short."

"And the missing ewes were never found?" Harriet asked, her mind racing. November was the month before Simon Boyes had returned to the area. Did that mean he wasn't responsible for any of the disappearances? On the other hand, perhaps the more recent losses had nothing to do with one from a few months before.

"Not that I ever heard."

"In my day," an elderly man muttered, "the sheep on the moors were so wild, a rustler would never have gotten them onto a trailer. Nowadays it's easy, since they're used to being trucked back and forth. When I was a lad, the shepherds and their dogs walked the sheep from field to field. Used to clog up the roads something fierce, I can tell you."

Others rose to leave, appearing keen to escape before the man embarked on a long story.

But Harriet loved hearing about the old ways of farming. "When were you born?"

"In 1938," he said proudly.

"So you lived through the Second World War. Do you remember it?"

"I was seven when it ended. We had three little'uns from London who lived with us for over a year too. I don't think they wanted to go back after the war. Loved country living, as does anyone with an ounce of sense. They kept in touch with my parents for years."

"You wouldn't happen to remember Samuel Bishop, a tenant farmer from the Kingsbury Estate?"

The man chuckled. "You've been listening to the village's ghost stories, haven't you, lass?"

"I suppose I have."

He nodded. "I didn't know the man myself. But I remember the storm right enough. Almost didn't make it home from school, the snow came down so hard and fast. When it was over, my dad took me and my brothers from farm to farm to help dig out sheep." The man shuddered. "Never seen the like since, thank the good Lord. Left a lot of folks devastated."

"Do you recall people speculating about what happened to Samuel Bishop?"

"Oh, aye. There'd been some strangers in town the week he disappeared. Government types, my parents said." He scratched his beard. "Maybe here to consider offering some sort of compensation scheme to the farmers who lost their flocks. Not that the government had two pence to rub together in those days. But farmers didn't have insurance, and the government couldn't afford to lose their farmers. They were having a hard enough time feeding the country. We were still on rations for years after the war, you know."

"I've heard that, yes."

"I wouldn't put much stock in the rumor they were foreign spies bent on finishing what the blizzard didn't. It's a wonder folks didn't accuse the Russians of seeding the storm in the first place. You

Yanks started that, you know. I remember my teacher talking about it in current events."

"We should get going," Aunt Jinny interjected. "Henry's waiting to lock up."

Harriet thanked the gentleman for sharing his stories and apologized to Henry for keeping him.

"No worries," he assured her. "We're happy to have you join us. I hope you'll come Friday night. The pastor always plans entertaining games."

"This Friday night?" Will's plan for their first Valentine's was a church event?

"Yes, it's our Valentine's Day Fete. We host one every year. All the information was in last Sunday's bulletin."

She hadn't seen that bulletin because she'd spent Sunday morning in a cow barn tending an ailing heifer.

"Do you think you'll come?" Elaine asked.

"I'll do my best," Harriet promised. Maybe Will had assumed she'd seen the bulletin and knew what he had planned for their evening.

Aunt Jinny paused outside her car. "If you want to put the kettle on when we get home, we could tackle that journal excerpt you need help decoding."

"That would be great."

Fifteen minutes later, Aunt Jinny tapped at the garden-side door before letting herself in with a plate of cookies in hand. "I thought we might need brain food."

"I seem to recall Anthony complaining that you'd make him eat 'brain food' of eggs before exams?" Harriet teased.

Aunt Jinny's eyes sparkled. "Stuff and nonsense. Your grandad spoiled him rotten with biscuits. He didn't need them from me. Now I get to spoil my grandkids and favorite niece. Call it making up for all the spoiling I didn't get to do while you were growing up on another continent."

Harriet gave her aunt a kiss on the cheek and helped herself to a cookie. "I love the way you think." She let Charlie and Maxwell out into the garden then poured the tea. "Did you want to work in here or in the office?"

"What exactly are we decoding?"

"I'm hoping they're breeding records."

"Then the office would be best. We may need to reference some of Dad's books."

"To be honest, I'm beginning to suspect I've set myself on a wild-goose chase to procrastinate writing the magazine article," Harriet said. "I'd hoped to find proof that Samuel Bishop worked on a secret government breeding project, since food continued to be scarce following the war. It sounded like a great idea Sunday night, but I've yet to find any evidence to support the rumors."

"Do you need it? Couldn't you simply use the historical story as a hook to illustrate that farmers have always faced challenges? Then focus on current success stories—farmers who've diversified to remain viable."

"That would be simpler. But I'd still like to see if you can figure out the journal pages I photographed." Harriet picked up their cups of tea and led the way to the office. "There's a chance Rowena's husband might secure some answers for me too. He said he'd see if he could find out whether Samuel Bishop worked for the government in the forties."

"Clive Talbot actually admitted to working for the government?" Aunt Jinny set the plate of biscuits on the desk and took up her tea.

Harriet smirked. "Not in so many words, no." She collected the printouts of the photos of the journal pages she'd taken and spread them on the desk. "These are the pages I'm hoping you can help me with. The farm manager at Kingsbury said that if they're breeding records, he doesn't recognize the codes."

"Which makes sense if Samuel wanted to keep the records secret." Aunt Jinny studied the first page. "This might not be a code at all. It resembles the shorthand Mum used in Dad's earliest record books." Aunt Jinny scanned the bookshelves. Finding what she wanted on the top shelf, she took down a ledger and opened it carefully. "Yes, right here." She rotated a page toward Harriet.

Harriet stared at the illegible scrawl. "Can you read it?"

"No, but I'm sure we can find a table for the symbols online."

Harriet switched on the computer and entered a search for shorthand symbols. After scanning a few entries, she groaned. "Apparently, there have been numerous shorthand versions over the years. Pitman or Gregg would've been the most likely one used here in the 1940s, but Nana would have used a modernized version."

"Do they have a table we can compare to the pages you photographed?"

"Yes, hold on a second. I'll print a couple of copies." Harriet collected the printouts from the printer and handed one to her aunt. "We'll divide and conquer."

"There's hardly any difference from one symbol to the next." Aunt Jinny pointed to the first jot at the top of her page. "I can't tell if this would be a *P*, *B*, *S*, or a *TH*."

"You're comparing them to the Gregg symbols?"

"Yes, I think they have the most matches."

"Me too." Harriet scrutinized the mark in question. "Although that one is identical to the *L* in the Pitman system. According to my research, in the early twentieth century, the Border Leicester was one of the most sought-after breeds for crossbreeding because it was the UK's largest indigenous sheep."

"In Gregg's system, the second letter would be an *O*."

Harriet's interest piqued. "That makes sense too. Lonks are the largest hill breed. And they've been raised in the Yorkshire Pennines for more than two centuries."

"Okay, so how about I transcribe what I think this page would look like if this is Pitman shorthand and you do it for Gregg? Then we'll see which one gives us information that makes the most sense?"

Pen in hand, Harriet set to work. "I have a bad feeling that in addition to shorthand, Samuel used his own code for the breeds."

"You said the livestock auction has records of sheep he bought and sold?"

"Yes."

"If we find them listed in his journal as well, we should be able to compare his list to the auction records to figure out the abbreviations he used for those breeds."

"That's brilliant, Aunt Jinny," Harriet said admiringly.

Aunt Jinny tilted her phone screen to show Harriet what she'd found online. "The Gregg system includes symbols for months, days, and numbers. Check out the symbols for March and April." She held her phone beside one of the printed journal pages. "Those look like the dates to me. They'd be the common months lambs would be born."

"You're right. I'd say the Gregg system is our winner. Let's each take a page and rewrite it using Gregg's system."

They soon grew adept at translating the symbols into letters, words, and numbers.

Sitting back, Harriet studied the page she'd finished. "If I'm deciphering this correctly, he took twins from crosses he'd made two years prior and mated each with a sire of a different breed. But based on the dates, the snowstorm likely claimed the ewes' lives before any lambs were born. How sad."

"It is," Aunt Jinny agreed. "I have some breed abbreviations I can't figure out."

Harriet took the paper from her aunt. "I'll compare this to the list of breeds I've compiled. My theory is that he started with hardy breeds that make good mothers and have easy lambing and then crossed them with larger sires."

Stifling a yawn, Aunt Jinny pushed back from the desk and stretched. "I recognized a couple of downland breeds listed too."

"We should call it a night." Harriet gathered all the pages together and tapped them against the desk to straighten the pile. "I appreciate your help with this."

"Happy to help. I enjoy puzzles."

Aunt Jinny headed home, and Harriet settled Maxwell and Charlie in for the night. As she plugged in her phone to charge it, she discovered three missed texts from Will.

Smiling, she keyed a response, sharing details of the evening's small group meeting.

I'M GLAD YOU HAD A GOOD TIME, he replied. I'M SORRY I WASN'T THERE. I WAS LOOKING FORWARD TO OUR TEA.

YOU WERE WHERE YOU NEEDED TO BE. YOU NEVER NEED TO APOLOGIZE TO ME FOR THAT, she assured him.

HOPEFULLY NEITHER OF US WILL HAVE AN EMERGENCY THAT DISRUPTS FRIDAY EVENING'S PLANS.

He must have assumed all along that she'd understood he planned to take her to the church fete. She texted a happy face emoji with ELAINE SAID YOU ALWAYS PLAN ENTERTAINING GAMES.

DON'T WORRY. I PROMISE NOT TO ENTANGLE YOU IN ANY EMBARRASSING ONES.

How had they gone from *entertaining* to *embarrassing*? Now she was worried.

CHAPTER ELEVEN

Harriet hoped to fall asleep as soon as her head hit the pillow, but her mind was having none of it. If she wasn't imagining what kind of embarrassing games she might be subjected to at a Valentine's Day church fete, she was contemplating the possibility of foreign powers being so determined to halt a secret breeding program that they'd play God with the weather. That alone was proof of how tired she was.

Finally, she gave up trying to sleep and padded downstairs to her grandfather's study. She quickly reviewed lab results that must have come in after she left the clinic that afternoon and made notes to Polly on which animals would need follow-up appointments.

Next she opened her research file for the magazine article and jotted down a few of the extra details the man from church had supplied, including the speculation about cloud seeding causing the uncharacteristic storm that killed thousands of sheep across the county. It would certainly provide an interesting flavor, if nothing else. But her thoughts kept straying to the spate of disappearing sheep.

Harriet made a note to herself to ask at the farmers association meeting if any others had experienced similar losses. Given the news of Mr. Vail's loss back in November, the situation could be far more widespread than anyone realized. In a community where everyone seemed to know everyone else's comings and goings, the fact something like this could happen right under their noses with no one talking about it was nothing short of remarkable.

She typed *sheep rustling in the UK* into her computer's web browser. The multitude of headlines that populated the page stunned her. From organized gangs taking large numbers of sheep to opportunists snatching one or two animals at a time, the sheer magnitude of the problem was mind-boggling—to say nothing of law enforcement's apparent inability to stop it.

She found it difficult to believe that rustlers loading hundreds of sheep into a tractor-trailer could slip away unnoticed by anyone, let alone offload the sheep without arousing suspicion. But she supposed organized gangs would have a complicit recipient lined up— one they'd sufficiently bribed to turn a blind eye to any hint that false documentation had been supplied with the animals. Never mind that they could be selling meat unfit for consumption.

People buying meat at a cut-rate price under the table should know they would get what they paid for. Clearly, they weren't averse to taking that risk. But how many others along the supply chain were unwittingly affected? Like the diner who didn't know their favorite restaurant bought its meat on the cheap.

Despite all the stories about organized gangs, the few arrests that had been made amounted to odd opportunists with lousy luck, like the men pulled over for a routine traffic stop found to have a bleating sheep in their back seat. Or the farmer who was caught selling another farmer's stock at auction. In fact, the majority of the successfully prosecuted cases involved thieves connected to the farming community. It was little wonder that farmers were reluctant to make a big to-do about one or two missing sheep. The farming community surrounding White Church Bay were good folk, the kind of folk who'd be reluctant to cast aspersions on a fellow farmer.

She winced at the memory of how quickly she'd done exactly that with Mr. Wilcox.

After making notes on the security measures police and vendors suggested farmers take to deter future thefts, Harriet smothered a yawn as she checked the clock. It was almost midnight. If she didn't want to yawn her way through the farmers association meeting tomorrow night, she had better get some shut-eye. She had no idea if they'd be open to her addressing the group, but she hoped to raise awareness of the current problem. Perhaps they would be able to prevent future thefts, if thefts were indeed the cause of the missing sheep.

Way too few hours later, a dairy farmer's emergency call summoned her from bed. Reviewing the symptoms he listed over the phone, Harriet had a tentative diagnosis in mind before she pulled on her boots. Her examination confirmed her suspicions.

"I'll need to perform a small procedure ASAP, but then she'll be fine," she assured the farmer.

He nodded in stoic Yorkshire fashion. "Get on with it."

She didn't take his gruff tone personally. She could tell by his pained expression that the whole ordeal caused him more anguish than the cow.

Repositioning himself near the cow's head, he talked her through the procedure while Harriet worked. Despite the large size of his dairy herd, he clearly cared for each of his "lasses" as individuals. That was Harriet's favorite kind of client—one who would notice an issue and immediately bring the vet in to give the animal the best possible chance of recovery.

Thankfully, Harriet managed to finish the entire procedure in under an hour. "She shouldn't have any more trouble," she said as she washed up and gathered her equipment. "Was there anything else before I go?"

She'd learned that Yorkshire farmers appreciated getting as much as they could from a vet's farm visit.

"Nay. First calves aren't due till March."

"If you have any concerns, don't hesitate to call. Better that we catch a situation early like you did this morning."

"Thanks, Doc." The farmer's bright blue eyes displayed the gratitude he seemed unable to put into words.

By the time Harriet returned to Cobble Hill, Polly had arrived. "Would you mind sterilizing the equipment I used this morning and restocking the Beast so I can grab a quick shower?" Harriet asked her.

"No problem." Polly consulted her cell phone. "You have twenty minutes until your first appointment."

"That's plenty." By the time Harriet finished and raced downstairs, Polly had a steaming cup waiting for her in the kitchen along with two cherry muffins.

"I went on a baking spree last night," she explained.

"After your decorating spree? The reception area is lovely, by the way."

Polly winced. "After the way I tried to abandon my post when Van was here, I was feeling a bit guilty." She ducked her head. "I worked at

Galloway's one summer as a teen, and their rule was 'No foul moods in the shop.' A rule I probably needed to be reminded of."

"Nonsense. You haven't been that moody. A little sad, but that's natural. We're friends, Polly. I don't expect you to be a robot here."

"Van must hate me now. He scarcely spoke to me yesterday. Do you think I was stupid to refuse his proposal?"

"No, I understand that it was too soon for you. And I think he does too. You both need some time. But you know what?"

"What?" Polly lifted her gaze, hope glimmering in her eyes.

"I think he's the kind of guy who'd agree that it's a woman's prerogative to change her mind." Harriet struggled to contain the smile tugging at her lips.

"Do you really think so?"

"I do." Harriet winked.

Laughing, Polly swiped at her damp eyes. Apparently, being reassured that her reaction to his proposal hadn't carved her future love life—or lack thereof—in stone had unleashed a swell of repressed emotions.

"Take all the time you need." Harriet scooped up a muffin to go with her coffee and headed to the waiting area. "I'll check in our first patient."

Doreen arrived later that morning, clearly hoping for a quick chat.

Harriet invited her next client to wait for her with his pet budgie in the exam room before turning her attention to Doreen. "What's wrong? Please don't tell me more sheep have gone missing."

"No, thank goodness. I wanted to thank you for telling Van about our tup. It honestly hadn't occurred to us that Prince Charming might have been stolen. We were so certain he'd wandered off on his own. If it had been one of our lead girls missing, we would've thought it strange that the others didn't follow. They usually do, the daft things. They'd follow each other right off a cliff. But they don't tend to follow the rams."

"You don't need to thank me," Harriet protested. "With half-term break starting this weekend, you must have a million and one things to do."

"I do, but I baked hundreds of scones for the week and exhausted the room in my freezer. I was wondering if you had some to spare."

"Absolutely. Go on through to the kitchen and squeeze in whatever you can. I promise not to steal any." She grinned. "As tempting as it would be."

Doreen handed her a small container. "These are for you and Polly to enjoy, with my compliments."

Harriet gave her neighbor a warm hug. "You're the best. Thank you. Oh, Doreen, did Van know about the Vails' missing sheep?"

"I brought that up with him. It's funny that a connection between all the incidents never occurred to me when Prince Charming went missing. Not until Van asked if we thought he might've been nicked."

"Well, hopefully the stolen van they recovered will provide the lead needed to catch the culprit." Harriet said goodbye to Doreen and collected the waiting budgie's file from the reception desk then hurried to the exam room. "Thanks for waiting, Mr. Yates. Now what seems to be the problem with Griffin?"

"He's not eating. He knocks his food every which way about the cage but never seems satisfied."

Harriet assessed the bird. "His overgrown beak is likely hampering his ability to eat."

"I told the wife his beak didn't look right. Can you help him?"

"I'll trim the beak, and he should be as good as new."

Mr. Yates eyed the bird. "Don't know how you hope to catch him."

"There's a nifty trick for that." She rummaged through the cupboard for a tiny headlamp and fit it on her head. Next, she closed the blinds and shut off the room lights. "Budgies don't see well in the dark." Harriet opened the cage and easily caught the bird, murmuring gently to him when he squeaked in protest. "It's okay, Griffin. This won't hurt a bit." Harriet gave the beak a neat trim before popping him back into the cage. She switched on the room lights once more.

"That was brilliant."

Harriet smiled. "If he continues to have issues, don't hesitate to call. But I'm confident the overgrown beak was to blame. Supplying him with a cuttlebone or mineral block and branches will also help him keep it trimmed."

"Brilliant," the budgie echoed, and they both burst into laughter.

A lull in appointments early that afternoon gave Harriet time to create a list of concerns she wanted to raise at the farmers association meeting if given the chance. Perhaps the meeting would give her insights that could help crack the sheep-rustling case. And she wouldn't mind getting some input for her magazine article.

When Will called to ask her to tea minutes before Dierdre was due to arrive, Harriet reluctantly declined.

"I understand," he said when she told him about the farmers association meeting. "I should be working on Sunday's sermon anyway."

"We don't want anyone accusing me of keeping you from your clerical duties," Harriet teased.

"Good thing they can't see how often my mind wanders over to Cobble Hill Farm then."

Harriet's cheeks warmed. "Perhaps you should get a dog. Then you'd have an excuse to wander about here in person."

"Seeing you is excuse enough for me. If the weather would only cooperate."

"I'll say. Does the sun ever shine around here this time of year? The other night, I actually researched the stats. Did you know the UK averages seventy-two hours of sunshine in February? I'm seriously considering buying a full-spectrum light and plugging it into the Beast for my drives from farm to farm."

Will chuckled. "On the next sunny day we'll have to play hooky for a couple of hours and take a walk in the sunshine."

"Sounds like a plan. For now, though, I'm afraid I need to go. I'm expecting Dierdre any minute."

"Wait, would you like me to pick you up tomorrow evening?"

"I'd better drive myself. I never know when an emergency might arise."

"Okay. See you at seven then."

"Yes, take care." Disconnecting the call, Harriet rolled her eyes. *Take care?* Was that the best she could come up with? But it was way too soon to say *love you.* Never mind how many months she'd felt the emotional tug to explore the possibility of being more than friends.

Now that it was happening, it was almost as if she was getting a weird case of cold feet. Maybe Aunt Jinny was right that she was totally overthinking the whole thing. She should relax and go with the flow.

That might be easier if it weren't the eve of what was supposed to be the most romantic day of the year.

When Harriet was little, Dad had always been oblivious to the dates, so her ever-practical mom finally suggested they celebrate the occasion after the official day. It was a win-win solution. The pressure was off Dad. Babysitters and dinner reservations were easier to get. And they got to enjoy sale-price chocolate and flowers, which suited her deal-loving mom better than an overpriced bouquet arriving at the door on Valentine's Day.

Harriet supposed she should be happy that a guy's expectations of the day weren't typically as elaborate as a woman's. Was Will obsessing over how to make the day special for her when they'd be sharing it with half the church? She didn't want him to feel obligated to make a grand gesture he wasn't truly ready for. At the same time, she thought she would be disappointed if he didn't at the very least give her a card. But if even she didn't know what her own expectations were, how was he supposed to meet them?

The sound of Dierdre's voice in the waiting room was a welcome interruption. Thank goodness the stupid holiday would be over in less than thirty-six hours. Then she and Will could carry on with getting to know each other at their own pace.

The remainder of the afternoon flew by while she made farm calls with Dierdre.

Buckling herself into the truck after helping Harriet administer the TB tests on the Andersons' small dairy herd, Dierdre said, "We made good time. Do you think we'll be done early enough to attend the farmers association meeting tonight?"

"That's the plan." Harriet started the Land Rover and wasted no time getting on the road. "We have one call left—a goat that appears to be going blind." Harriet listed the symptoms the farmer reported and asked Dierdre for her theories.

"An eye infection?" Dierdre thumbed the information into her phone. "This online vet manual says an ocular rupture can lead to blindness. Does that mean we're already too late?"

"Not necessarily. So far, we only have Mrs. Barnes's description to go on. She may have assumed Billy was blind due to the loss of iris color when he isn't."

"To be fair, I'd probably think the same thing."

Driving into the farmyard, Harriet spotted Billy the goat, a repeat patient who was known to be a bit mischievous, and parked by the fence nearest to him.

Felicity Barnes came around the barn leading an adorable Hampshire Down with black face and feet.

"Oh, wow," Dierdre exclaimed. "That's the cutest sheep I've ever seen."

Felicity's countenance brightened. "This is Bo Peep. And she took first prize in last year's fair. We plan to breed her this November."

Harriet's chest squeezed at the thought of Prince Charming, who'd taken a prize at that same fair. "You should have no trouble with her. Hampshires are known for trouble-free lambing."

"How old is she?" Dierdre asked.

"About a year."

While the pair chatted about which breed Felicity might use for a sire, Harriet slipped into the pasture with Billy and began her examination. An odd feeling of being watched prickled the back of her neck. She glanced over her shoulder to make sure Felicity hadn't added a new animal to her menagerie that might get it into his head to charge her. Seeing nothing, she continued her examination. But the sensation grew stronger.

Straightening, Harriet scanned the far fence line and bristled at the sight of a familiar figure. "What's Simon Boyes doing here?"

CHAPTER TWELVE

Harriet didn't take her eyes off Simon as Felicity explained, "We hired the lad to mend that fence, on Pastor Will's recommendation."

"I see." Biting back the temptation to caution the woman about hiring a wolf to mind the sheep, Harriet returned her attention to the ailing goat. "It looks like Billy has some inflammation in his eyes. Has he pulled one of his escape-artist pranks recently? He might've picked up an infection from other animals."

Felicity scowled at the goat. "Didn't I tell you your walkabouts were going to get you killed one day?" To Harriet, Felicity added, "He escaped a few days ago. Again. That's why I hired Simon to mend the fence."

"Good. I'll give Billy an antibiotic injection and a mineral injection. But the condition is highly contagious, so you need to keep him away from your other animals. Frequently wiping his eyes will help to deter flies from bothering him and potentially carrying the infection to your other animals. If you could fetch me a bucket of warm water and soap, I'll clean his eyes before administering the injection."

As Felicity hurried off, Dierdre whispered, "Isn't Simon Boyes the bloke Polly thinks nicked the van? Why would the pastor recommend him for a job?"

"I imagine Simon needed the work and Felicity needed someone to do it." Harriet prepared the injection, doing her best to not betray her feelings. Reminding herself that the first sheep theft happened in November before Simon returned to White Church Bay, she added, "Pastor Will believes in giving others second chances."

"That's good of him, I guess. I've heard that some people just need an opportunity to turn over a new leaf."

Except given how much Simon was loafing about, he didn't appear to be making the most of his second chance. And maybe the sheep that went missing in November had nothing to do with the recent thefts.

Harriet pushed down her ungracious attitude. "I don't suppose he'd be foolish enough to steal from Felicity when he'd be the first one the police would suspect."

"That's true enough," Dierdre agreed. "And I would think a smart rustler would go after sheep from a field full of them, where a few missing ones wouldn't be noticed."

Harriet fought the urge to march up to Simon and demand to know where he really was Sunday. Except she doubted his story would change from the vague response he'd given Will that night. Besides, she wasn't sure if it would be better if Simon knew they were onto him or not. Maybe she should suggest to Van that he tail Simon in the evening. Perhaps the DC would even catch him in the act. Then again, remembering how she'd already falsely accused Mr. Wilcox, maybe she shouldn't say anything to Van at all.

After they'd finished treating the goat and were driving back to the clinic, Dierdre said, "By the way, I asked Tris what he was doing near the Fairburns' place the other afternoon. He said it wasn't him. That I mistook someone with a similar dog for him."

"Do you think that's possible?" Harriet asked. "There must've been something else familiar about who we saw to make you think he was Tristan."

"He wore the same kind of long, waxed coat Tris wears on wet days. But he had his hood up because it was drizzling, so I didn't see his face. Plus, we saw him from a distance in a moving vehicle."

Harriet nodded, but her gut wasn't ready to let her take Tristan's word for it. She hated how distrustful these thefts had made her. One second she was thinking Van should tail Simon, and the next she was thinking Dierdre's brother knew more than he was admitting. What was wrong with her? Twice Tristan had willingly dropped what he was doing to help them search for Prince Charming. Surely he would have stayed as far away as possible if he'd taken the sheep or knew who had.

And yet, until they found out who was actually behind the thefts, how could she rule anyone out for certain?

The farmers at the meeting gave Harriet a warm welcome. Wooden folding chairs were lined up to face the risers that served as a stage, but most of the attendees were still milling about and catching up on one another's news while they enjoyed home-baked treats and hearty tea.

When the president of the association stepped to the podium and called the meeting to order, Harriet slipped into a chair in the back row and shifted from side to side in an effort to spot Dierdre. But there was no sign of her. Harriet scanned the front row, trying to determine which farmer might be Dierdre's boyfriend. There were more young men here than she'd expected. But only one paid more attention to his lap than to the president—Reggie reviewing his notes, maybe?

"Perhaps White Church Bay's newest vet could speak to that question," the president said, and Harriet looked up to see all eyes turned in her direction.

Her heart jolted. "I'm sorry. What was the question?"

The president shifted his mouth closer to the mic. "Are you, or do you know of any other vets in the area who will be participating in the new Annual Health and Welfare Review the government is funding?"

Harriet stood. "Yes, I am. The program provides for an annual visit, meant to be an opportunity to focus on the specific health and welfare priorities for your livestock."

The president nodded encouragingly. "It sounds like an excellent opportunity to build a working relationship with our newest vet." His eyes crinkled with his broad smile. "And I'd like to take this opportunity to welcome Dr. Harriet Bailey to our farming community, though I think most of us know her by now."

Harriet ducked her head under all the attention but murmured her thanks. Then she remembered the subject she wanted to raise at the meeting. When the applause subsided, she asked, "Would it be okay if I brought up a topic for discussion?"

"By all means," the president said.

"Several prizewinning sheep have gone missing over the past couple of weeks, and the police are concerned that sheep rustlers could be active in the area."

Chaos erupted.

One of Harriet's clients announced that he'd discovered a few sheep missing that morning. A few others made similar reports, while still more clamored about the wrongness of it all. Harriet wondered if it was significant that year-old sheep rather than in-lamb ewes were taken. Could be they were simply an easier target, being in pastures farther afield than ewes close to giving birth. This time of year, they'd also be the nearest to lamb-quality meat a rustler would find in these parts.

Harriet raised her voice above the din. "If we want to see to it that rustlers can't get away with plundering the local flocks, we'll need to work together. Report suspicious behavior, as well as strange vehicles parked along the road."

"Our farmhand installed infrared beams across our gates after an incident with some careless tourists last year," an older woman chimed in. "It sends an alert to my mobile if the beam is broken. They aren't cheap, but the peace of mind is worth it."

"My gimmers don't pasture anywhere near our house," another farmer grumbled. "A gizmo like that wouldn't do me any good. The trespassers would be long gone by the time I got there."

The president called for order, and the audience quieted.

"I don't want to create alarm or mistrust," Harriet continued. "Logistically speaking, it's impossible to keep a constant eye on your flocks. There are a few steps you can take, however, that might deter a would-be rustler." She detailed several suggestions she'd read about.

A young fellow near the front called, "A mate of mine in the Cotswolds had sheep stolen last year. Since then, he's been using a special microdot-embedded fleece paint. If someone scans the sheep, the info in the microdots allows them to trace the owners."

"So we might get our sheep back, but they'll have picked up who knows what diseases," another farmer growled.

The volume in the room rose with every new opinion added to the dialogue.

Finally, the president tabled the discussion. "But *do* report missing animals. I think the point Dr. Bailey wished to make is that when only one or two sheep go missing, it's easy to assume they wandered off. And while that could be what's happened, the police can't form an accurate picture of the situation if we don't report our losses."

Harriet mouthed her thanks to the man, who acknowledged her response with an affirming nod.

He then called up Walter Devon from the Ministry of Agriculture to field questions about applying for the Sustainable Farming Incentive, in which the government awarded funds to farmers for improving their land and work for the environment.

The questions and lively debate that ensued gave Harriet a renewed appreciation for the multitude of hats farmers had to wear to keep their farms viable. She'd chosen a timely topic for her magazine article. She should start writing it, rather than continue to waste her time trying to piece together the true Samuel Bishop story. Perhaps Walter would be able to give her the lowdown on a scenario that would make an even stronger hook for the article.

At last, the president invited Reggie Springfield, Diedre's boyfriend, to the podium to talk about the exciting results of his new worming approach compared to the efficacy of the established procedure.

Harriet couldn't help but chuckle. No one besides livestock farmers and vets would find anything about worming exciting.

The handsome, dark-haired young man spoke with confidence and authority, with an obvious mastery of his subject.

Dierdre slipped into the room a few minutes into his talk and took the seat beside Harriet's.

"Everything okay?" Harriet whispered. "I was worried you weren't going to make it."

"Sorry." Dierdre slid her arms from her dripping-wet coat and hung it over the back of her chair. "How's he doing?"

"He makes a compelling case for his approach."

"Do you agree with him?"

Someone in front of them twisted around and shushed them, sparing Harriet from having to give an opinion.

To Reggie's credit, he presented the pros and cons for both approaches. Then he showed the data he'd kept for both before and after he'd changed his methods. But what impressed Harriet the most was his passion for his animals' welfare. Dierdre had found herself an impressive beau.

The crowd must have agreed, because the applause was deafening when he finished. The president invited questions, and several hands shot up.

Harriet leaned closer to Dierdre. "He seems like a smart guy. I'm glad I came to hear him. It's great to see farmers sharing their knowledge and experiences with one another." Too bad Samuel Bishop had been prohibited from sharing anything with his fellow farmers. Unless...

Harriet's pulse quickened. What if he'd needed to call a vet to see to one of the sheep? It might have even been her great-grandfather. Cecil Bailey had started the veterinary practice at Cobble Hill before the outbreak of the Second World War, so he would have been well established in the community by 1947. Why hadn't she thought to check his records?

"And Reggie believes in modernization." Dierdre's remark drew Harriet from her thoughts. "He's saving for a specialized sheep-handling system now. He says it'll make deworming procedures much faster, safer, and easier."

"He's right. Tim Vail has one on his farm and runs his flock through worming and feet checks in no time. Perhaps we can drive to Reggie's farm sometime so you can give me a tour."

"I'll mention it to him. I'm sure he would be fine with it. He loves talking about his innovations and his farm." Dierdre's gaze strayed to the front of the room where Reggie was still deep in conversation with a pair of farmers. "As soon as he's free, I'll introduce you."

"That would be great." Harriet noticed the Ministry of Agriculture man sidling toward the door. "Excuse me a minute. I want to catch Walter Devon before he leaves."

The balding man greeted Harriet with a firm handshake. "Clive Talbot mentioned I might see you here."

A frisson of nervous energy zipped up her spine. "He spoke to you about my interest in Samuel Bishop?"

"He did. And I must admit, the story piqued my curiosity. It happened long before my time, of course, but I was able to confirm that your assumption is at least partially correct. The government did encourage research into breeding hardier, meatier sheep with better feed-conversion rates."

"But did the government officially work with Samuel Bishop?"

"That would've been before digital recordkeeping, so it's doubtful we could easily locate the answer for you. It would likely take more time than I suspect you have."

Reaching into her bag, she retrieved the pages she and her aunt had transcribed the night before. "Could you look at these and tell me if you think his approach would've been a novel strategy for the late 1940s?"

Devon perused the pages, stroking his bristled chin. "I can't attest to it being novel, but it is insightful. In theory, by using hardy breeds with minimum birthing issues and crossing them with larger breeds, he'd achieve a nice balance between minimizing losses while producing faster-growing lambs." He snapped a picture of one of the pages with his cell phone. "A couple of these breeds are almost extinct these days, out of favor with the introduction of imports. I can assign an intern to do a county flock records search for anything comparable. No promises, though."

"I understand. Anything you can find would be appreciated."

Harriet bid him goodbye then scanned the remaining farmers enjoying animated conversations around her. She wouldn't get another chance to talk to so many of them in one place again before her article was due, so she should take advantage of the opportunity.

Notepad in hand, she ventured from group to group, asking about the creative approaches the farmers used to stay profitable. Three hosted B&Bs while one rented out a special-event venue. Several incorporated farm shops on their land, others had planted trees for carbon tax credit payments, while still more hosted tours or birthday parties.

When she reached Dierdre and Reggie, she found them in a heated discussion. Harriet held back, not wanting to interrupt.

Dierdre spotted her and beckoned to her. "Here she is. I'll introduce you," she said to Reggie.

Reggie smiled amiably as he extended his hand. "Great to finally meet you. Dierdre talks about your exploits all the time."

His handshake was firm and his gaze direct. He had an aura of being wise beyond his years. Harriet could see why Dierdre was so taken with him. "She speaks fondly of you too," Harriet said. "Your presentation was very well done."

"I'm glad you approve. I'm sorry I can't visit longer. My grandfather texted that one of our first-time mothers is in labor, so I'm anxious to get home."

"Of course."

"Nice meeting you." He kissed Dierdre's cheek. "I'll talk to you later."

After he left, Dierdre seemed uncharacteristically subdued.

"What's wrong?" Harriet asked.

Dierdre shrugged. "He's not keen on my bringing you to the farm. Since it's lambing season, he's more obsessed with biosecurity than ever. He doesn't want me to go into his barns after I've been to other farms with you either."

"That's all right. Being careful is a good thing. I'm sure he'll be far too preoccupied with lambing to want to take time to give me a farm tour."

"I think hearing about more sheep disappearances is playing on his mind too," Dierdre said. "He can't afford to lose a single sheep, whether to lambing difficulties or to rustlers."

Harriet had heard the same sentiment expressed by more than one farmer that evening. "Hopefully, the heightened awareness generated tonight will help the police catch the culprit."

But she was beginning to fear that it was already too late for Prince Charming. The Danbys' beloved ram might be long gone by now.

CHAPTER THIRTEEN

Friday morning dawned sunny and bright, and Harriet took it as a good sign for the day.

The previous night, she'd skimmed through the faded notes in her great-grandfather's records without finding a single reference to Samuel Bishop or the Kingsbury Estate. Then she'd spent the rest of the evening mulling over a strategy to catch the sheep rustler—and getting nowhere. Finally, she'd devoted a good hour to worrying about the potential awkwardness of celebrating Valentine's Day with Will at church. Would he even let on that they were officially dating? Did she want him to? And if he didn't, how awkward would that be, to be single at a couples' party?

Scolding herself for dropping back into that spiral first thing in the morning, she jumped out of bed and grabbed the ringing phone.

"My ewe's gone blind," Mr. Aimes blurted. "Can you come straightaway?"

Harriet hurried out of the house. The sight of blue skies and the cheerful sound of robins singing lightened her heart once more. She'd first endeared herself to the Aimes family when their son, Allen, had brought a hen with a broken leg to her. She'd fixed the leg, and Rosie the hen expressed her gratitude by laying double-yolk eggs.

Harriet's cell phone rang as she started the Land Rover. Bracing herself for a busier morning than she'd anticipated, she answered the call without looking at the caller ID.

"Hey." Will's pleasant voice hummed through her vehicle. "The sun's shining."

She grinned like an idiot. "Yes, it is."

"Do you have time for a ramble this morning?"

"I might. I'm heading to a farm call at the moment and will have to check the appointment list when I return to the clinic. Can I call you then?"

"Sounds good. Talk to you later."

Harriet parroted him, sounding like Mr. Yates's mimicking budgie. She rolled her eyes at the schoolgirl nervousness that had gripped her the instant she'd heard Will's voice.

Driving to the farm, she focused her attention on the problem at hand. There were several conditions that could cause blindness in sheep. And, unlike with Billy, chances were that this animal's condition was very real and potentially permanent.

Mr. Aimes met her halfway across the driveway. "I took her into the barn. Over here." He led Harriet into the structure then motioned to a heavily pregnant ewe, who startled at his voice and bumped into the side of her penned area. Then she promptly lay down in the hay.

"How long has she been like this?"

"I noticed it this morning when she refused to eat at breakfast. She's not due until next week."

"Judging by her size, she's expecting twins. Is that right?"

"Aye." He jutted his chin toward the brightly colored fleece paint that marked the ewe's flank with how many lambs she was expecting. "It's her first pregnancy too. That's why I've been keeping a close eye on her."

Harriet caught a whiff of the ewe's breath. It was sweet. "I believe this is twin lamb disease. The extra demands of the pregnancy on her body have caused her blood sugar to drop dangerously low. If you hadn't called me, it could have killed her in less than twenty-four hours."

"But you can help her?" Mr. Aimes asked.

"How close to lambing is she?"

"Four days, give or take."

"That's good. The sooner she's due, the better her chances. I have some injections that will help her manage until then, and we have additional treatments as well. She should be fine." As Harriet administered the injections, she gave Mr. Aimes more instructions to help the pregnant ewe until she delivered.

"Will do," he said. "Appreciate you coming straight over."

"I'm glad you called when you did. You have a fine flock here."

"Aye," the man agreed with obvious pride.

"Are they all accounted for? The police are concerned sheep rustlers might be working the area."

The man's face blanched. "I hadn't heard that. I've been watching the pregnant ones closely, but I rent grazing land farther afield for the others. I'll check on them today."

"Good idea. If you come up short, let DC Worthington know."

"Will do. Cheers."

Harriet arrived at Cobble Hill to find Will's silver Kia Picanto parked outside the clinic. She hurried inside but found no sign of him.

"Where's Will?" she asked Polly.

"Wandering around outside." She pointed to a vase of red roses on the reception desk. "He brought those for you."

Harriet's heart pounded. Her hand shook as she reached for the card with the bouquet. It said simply, *Happy Valentine's Day. Love, Will.*

She swallowed hard. This was the first time either of them had used the word *love*. If she'd gotten around to signing the card she'd bought for him, she would have labored a long time over whether it was too soon to sign it that way.

The jingle of the bell over the clinic door made her whirl on the spot, bringing her face-to-face with Will. "Good morning. Thank you for the roses. They're beautiful."

"I'm glad you like them. Polly says your first appointment isn't until nine thirty, so I was hoping you'd join me for a walk until then."

"I'd love to." Harriet pretended not to notice Polly's suspiciously moist eyes, knowing today must be especially hard on her. "Polly, I'll have my phone with me, so you can call if there's an emergency."

"Sure thing. Enjoy yourself."

Will twined his fingers between Harriet's as they ambled through the field behind Aunt Jinny's cottage to the cliff trail.

Stopping to admire the view, Harriet inhaled the crisp sea air. "We aren't the only ones playing hooky."

Far below, people were taking advantage of the tide being out to enjoy a sunny walk along the rocky shoreline.

Harriet and Will took the trail away from White Church Bay. Passing through a tract of woodland, they found themselves surrounded by a carpet of snowdrops. Harriet gasped at the sight. "They're beautiful."

"Our first harbinger of spring." Will plucked a delicate bloom and tucked it behind her ear. Her heart skipped a bit.

They strolled in silence through the woodland, enjoying the sounds of nature—the chirping birds, the gentle breeze whispering in the treetops, the distant bleating of sheep. As they emerged from the canopy of trees, Harriet closed her eyes and lifted her face to the sun's warmth. "I needed this."

Will squeezed her hand. "Are you still beating yourself up over the Danbys' tup?"

"I'm fairly confident Dusty wasn't to blame, given the other disappearances and the stolen van."

Will stopped, pulling her to a halt beside him. "What stolen van?"

"The Galloways' old transport van was stolen over the weekend and abandoned in Whitby. Van thinks it might've been used in the sheep thefts."

Will's furrowed brow made her think his suspicions had veered in the same direction hers had when she'd first heard the news—to Simon Boyes.

Harriet bit her lip. "Sorry. I meant to tell you, but it slipped my mind." She cringed at the thought of what she needed to add. "And Van knows about Simon's previous car theft charge. He planned to talk to him."

"I see." Will resumed walking. "I guess it's only natural Simon would be one of their first suspects."

"He was in Whitby Sunday night," Harriet reminded him. "And I saw him with another guy on the street Tuesday night, flashing a wad of cash."

"You think he's the thief?"

"He sure acted like he had something to hide when you talked to him Sunday night."

"Aye." The conversation detour had dampened Will's mood as quickly as if a storm cloud had opened up over their heads.

Harriet checked the time on her phone. "We should probably start back."

"Aye. I'd like to pay Simon a visit."

Harriet opened her mouth to suggest the police might prefer he didn't. But she closed it again. Maybe Will could get through to the young man in a way the police might not be able to.

"I'm sorry the walk didn't pan out as cheerful as I'd hoped," Will said as they neared the house.

"I get it. You don't want to think you misjudged Simon. And maybe you haven't. Maybe the rest of us have."

"I know him well enough to know he didn't tell us the whole truth Sunday night. But I wouldn't have believed Ian would go along with covering up anything criminal."

Harriet gave Will's hand an encouraging squeeze. "If anyone can get the truth of Simon's involvement—or lack thereof—I'm sure you can. It would certainly be nice to see Prince Charming recovered before the weekend, if it's still possible."

Will's expression softened. "I'll see what I can unearth." He hugged her then started toward his car. "See you tonight."

"Looking forward to it." Though she couldn't help wondering if their stroll might have ended less abruptly if she hadn't mentioned the stolen vehicle.

At the sight of a police cruiser pulling into the driveway, Harriet paused at the clinic entrance. When she saw Van at the wheel, her hopes surged that he'd come with good news. Maybe she could spare Will from feeling the need to confront Simon.

Van parked in the car park and strode toward her, a single yellow rose in his hand.

Harriet's hopes deflated. "I guess this means you're not here with news about the thefts." She opened the clinic door for him.

"Nay, I am." He reached over her head to hold the door and motioned for her to enter first. "Thanks to whatever you said at last night's meeting, we had three more reports this morning of recent sheep disappearances—from Digger's, Barrowby's, and McGregor's farms."

"I can't believe it's taken this long for them to realize they were robbed."

"No one's been talking about it."

When Van followed Harriet into the clinic, Polly surged to her feet. Like a deer caught in the headlights of an oncoming car, her gaze fixed on the flower he held.

Harriet stayed by the entrance, not wanting to get in the way.

Van thrust the yellow rose at Polly. "This is for you. I know this situation isn't easy for either of us. Especially today. But I wanted you to know I'm still thinking of you."

Polly's gaze lifted to his. "Yellow is the color of friendship."

"It is. I hope we can figure out how to move forward, because I want to stay friends."

Polly's lips curved into a smile as she accepted the peace offering. "That's sweet of you. Thank you."

Van visibly relaxed. "You're welcome. I don't want you to feel uncomfortable around me."

She ducked her head. "I appreciate your concern."

Apparently conscientious about not overstaying his welcome, Van palmed his car keys and headed for the door.

"Wait," Harriet blurted. "Do you have any new leads on the sheep rustling?"

"Only what I told you."

"What about the stolen van? Did it yield any clues? Fingerprints?"

"Lots of prints, but none that were in the system. And the Galloways got in touch with their friends who'd been borrowing their van. They'd used it to transport goats, so that explains why there were signs of animals having been in it."

"There's no conclusive proof the van was used to transport stolen sheep?" Harriet clarified.

"No. But that doesn't mean it wasn't." He reached for the door then suddenly stopped. "I did ask about our police report archives for you. The chief said if you can find the report on Samuel Bishop, you're welcome to read it. He'll waive the required Request for Information form, since the files are so old. Someone from admin should have the 1947 boxes pulled from storage for you by the end of the day."

"That's awesome. Thank you."

"No problem. I hope you find what you're after."

Harriet's first client of the day arrived, and Van took that as his cue to exit.

Harriet sent the woman and her guinea pig ahead to an exam room then squeezed Polly's shoulder. "Are you okay?"

Polly held the yellow rose to her nose and inhaled deeply, her expression serene. "I'm better than I've been in a while. He is very sweet."

"I've always thought so."

"I do still want to be friends."

Harriet sensed an unspoken *maybe more* but kept the notion to herself and asked for their client's file.

Fifteen minutes later, she returned the file to Polly as a happier guinea pig and his owner exited the clinic. "The Case of the Limping Guinea Pig proved to be the Case of the Guinea Pig with a Splinter in His Paw. If only the mystery of the disappearing sheep was as simple to solve."

"I was thinking about that," Polly said. "If you don't count Tim Vail's case, did you notice that all the other sheep have gone missing in the last three weeks from farms that you visited in that time?"

Harriet stared at her, mentally reviewing the names Van had given her that morning. "I've been second-guessing myself over my visit to the Huckabys and Trussels, fearing I didn't secure the farm gates properly. But now that you mention it—you're right. That is kind of an uncomfortable coincidence. Do you think it's significant?"

Polly lowered her voice, even though the waiting room sat empty. "Dierdre also accompanied you on all those visits."

Harriet gasped. "You can't think Dierdre is a sheep rustler. She's too passionate about the animals, about becoming a vet. No way would she do anything to jeopardize her future."

"I agree. But she's also a chatterbox. What if she's being unwittingly tapped for information?"

"I've never taken her to the Danbys," Harriet countered.

"No, but Doreen has been by a couple of times when Dierdre's been here. Dierdre asked Doreen tons of questions about their farm. She's the most inquisitive person I've ever met, and I get the impression that she loves to share what she's learned."

"You might be onto something. We could be looking at a class-mate or her brother's friend. The one who drives the black van with tinted windows. It's possible the siblings are being used and don't even realize it."

"How do you think she'd react if you asked her who she tells about your vet visits?"

"I'm sure she won't be happy to think she could be a cog in the sheep-rustling scheme."

"Probably even less happy if she senses you suspect her brother," Polly mused.

Harriet remembered how readily Dierdre had accepted Tristan's denial of being near the Fairburns' place. His sister certainly wouldn't be a reliable witness when it came to vouching for him. "But considering how willing Tristan was to help us search for Prince Charming, I don't think he's involved. Now, his friend is another matter. He could be tapping Tristan for info that he innocently picks up from Dierdre's chatter at their dinner table."

Polly folded her arms over her chest. "Or Tristan could've been so quick to help precisely so that we *wouldn't* suspect him."

CHAPTER FOURTEEN

With an hour and a half to spare before she had to get ready for the Valentine's Day event at the church, Harriet headed to the police station, knowing she'd merely make herself a nervous wreck if she primped and preened all afternoon.

As promised, three boxes labeled *1947* awaited her at the station. She used a table in an empty interview room to go through them. Three-quarters of the way through the first box, she found Samuel's file.

Kingsbury Estate
April 1947

To Constable Wiggins's surprise, a wisp of smoke rose from the chimney of Samuel Bishop's hovel. Wiggins trekked through ankle deep mud to reach the door.

A squat, older woman answered his knock.

"Afternoon, ma'am. I'm Detective Sergeant Wiggins. Are you a relative of Samuel Bishop?"

"*Nay. Me and my husband took over tenancy here last week. No one's heard from Samuel going on a month now.*"

"*Aye, I'm investigating his disappearance. Did he leave anything behind?*"

"*They found his dog wandering the moors.*" The woman lowered her voice. "*It's what convinced his lordship the poor chap snuffed it out there. That dog never left Samuel's side.*"

"*Where is the dog now?*"

The woman motioned to the hills. "*Wandering the heath, I shouldn't wonder. I only see him when he's hungry.*"

"*Did Mr. Bishop leave any belongings in the house?*"

"*Not much. The estate manager collected the flock records. There were a few bits and bobs of clothing plus pots and plates and such. Nothing valuable, mind. The manager said it'd be all right for us to keep those.*"

Wiggins nodded. "*What about an address book? Correspondence?*"

"*Nothing like that.*"

"*Could you give me the names of his closest mates?*"

The woman shook her head. "*He had none that I know of. Kept to himself, he did. Although the last couple of years, folks say they'd noticed a dodgy bloke calling on him now and again.*" The woman smoothed her apron. "*I don't hold to such gossip. Samuel was a good Christian man, and no mistake.*"

"*This bloke you saw—*"

"*Nay, I never saw him. I heard folks talk about him. You know how folks gossip when they don't know what's what.*"

"So you don't know the bloke's name?"

"Nay." The woman sniffed the air. "My bread's going to burn if I don't fetch it out."

"Certainly. Thank you for your time."

The farmhands eyed Wiggins warily as he strode across the yard to the manager's office. He knew better than to read into their reticence. The Kingsbury Estate and nearby village were all but cut off from the rest of the world by the moors. Aside from those conscripted to fight in the war, most folks lived and died here, having never ventured more than ten or twenty miles from home in their lifetime.

When asked about the visitor to Samuel's farm, the estate manager said he'd last seen the chap after the carriageway was cleared following the blizzard. "He didn't stop at the main house, and Samuel wouldn't say what he wanted."

"When you cleared his house for the new tenants, did you find personal correspondence or money? Anything to suggest he'd been paid for the animals?"

The manager averted his gaze. "Nay."

Wiggins didn't believe him. Folks in these parts didn't trust banks. They kept what little they had inside their mattress or buried in a tin in the back garden. Not that it mattered. Finding a hidden stash wouldn't help him locate Bishop's body. But identifying the suspicious man the neighbors had seen might give him a lead.

Harriet flipped over the page and blinked. That was the extent of the report? No follow-up or additional interviews? No resolution? She thumbed through the other files but found nothing more. After returning the boxes, she expressed her frustration to the clerk.

"If Samuel Bishop had no loved ones, no one would've been pushing for answers, so his case might have been eclipsed by more pressing issues," the clerk said. "With no new leads, it went cold."

The statement saddened Harriet and fueled her determination to find out what really happened to the man. If the estate manager at the time had bothered to read Samuel's journals, he would have known the tenant farmer was secretly working with the government. Or had the estate manager deliberately withheld that from the constable because of rumors that his lordship entertained foreign spies?

Forcing herself to set aside her musing for the time being, Harriet returned home and dressed for her evening with Will. The butterflies fluttering in her stomach went into hyperdrive on the way to the church.

With Will in charge of the evening, she could wind up spending half the night sitting alone. And sitting alone in a roomful of happy couples sounded worse than sitting home alone watching a sappy movie curled up with Maxwell and Charlie on the couch. Worse than that, none of her closest friends would be there tonight. Polly definitely wouldn't be. The Danbys were bound to be too busy getting the farm ready for opening day tomorrow. Aunt Jinny was babysitting her grandchildren so Anthony and Olivia could go to the movies.

Harriet wrung her sweaty palms around the steering wheel as she reached the church. Apparently, everyone else in town had come to the dinner, because there wasn't a parking space to be had. Chastising herself for not coming earlier, Harriet circled the lot. Everyone would see her come in. Alone. How was she supposed to greet Will, the pastor she was newly and semisecretly dating, in front of his congregants?

A figure waved at her from outside the church, and she pulled up to speak to him. "Will?" She rolled down her window and caught a whiff of his cologne—sandalwood and pine. *Nice.*

"I'm glad I spotted you," he said. "I was watching for you, but I had to step inside for a second to help Mr. Jenkins on the stairs. You can park behind my car in the parsonage drive."

"Thanks. See you in a minute." She drove away and parked where he'd indicated. Pocketing her keys, she reached for the Valentine's Day card she'd brought for him then hesitated. Should she take it with her or give it to him later?

Her door opened, and her heart jolted. "Will! Sorry, I didn't realize you had followed me."

His broad smile calmed her nerves. "I couldn't let my valentine walk in alone." He offered her his hand.

"Would you like your card before we go in?"

His grin widened. "Sure."

Staying in the driver's seat, she handed him the card and watched his expression as he opened the envelope. He spent an inordinately long time admiring the cartoon picture on the front of the card—a pair of dogs with a heart floating over their heads.

"Cute." He opened the card and read the inside aloud. "'Dating you is like living in my very own *furry* tail.'" Will laughed. "I love it."

Harriet relaxed, pleased by his response.

He helped her from her seat and hugged her. "I'm so glad fairy tales always have happy endings."

Her heart soared as she rested her head against his shoulder. He made it sound as if she wasn't the only one who'd been contemplating the possibility of a happily-ever-after for them. And he seemed a whole lot more confident that it would happen.

Shifting to face the church, he took her hand. "Ready?"

"Ready as I'll ever be." Her steps slowed as they neared the front door, but Will didn't comment on her hesitation. In all the possible scenarios she'd fretted over, entering the church on his arm hadn't been among them, which was silly, considering she was his date.

Will held the door for her then reclaimed her hand as they stepped inside.

The parish hall was a riot of red and pink streamers and hearts. Round tables adorned with red tablecloths and colorful floral arrangements each held six elegant place settings. The room was abuzz with chattering couples, but a hush swept through as Will and Harriet entered, followed by fevered whispering. Harriet could practically feel the rumor mill grinding.

Will led her to a table at the front of the hall that was already occupied by two older couples—Elaine and Henry Dawson and Tamzin and Roger Pickers, owners of the local pet store. Tamzin, in her usual flair, wore a stunning fuchsia pantsuit with matching chunky jewelry that helped Harriet feel a little less conspicuous.

"Hello," Harriet greeted them.

"Harriet, my dear," Elaine gushed, "I didn't realize you and Will were dating. Why didn't you say something Wednesday evening?"

Heat rushed to her cheeks. "We've only been out a few times."

"Thanks to our unpredictable schedules," Will added with a warm smile. "It certainly hasn't been for a lack of trying."

Tamzin grinned as Harriet slipped into the seat beside her, then whispered, "Well done."

Harriet had always been a valued client at Tamzin's pet store and considered her a friend, especially since she'd helped the woman come clean about dognapping the village's star show dog. Tonight, Harriet appreciated her extra vote of confidence.

The catered roast chicken dinner with all the fixings was delicious, and the casual dinner conversation allayed Harriet's anxiety. Tamzin carried on about all things pet-store related, while her quiet husband indulged in seconds. Every so often, Tamzin would ask, "Isn't that right, Roger?" to which he'd dutifully respond, "Yes, Tamzin," then carry on eating.

Will, who'd been engaged in a side conversation with Henry about the church roof, must have realized that his table had finished eating. "I guess it's time to start the activities." He squeezed Harriet's hand then stood and strode to the front of the room. "Our first activity for the evening is a game called Name That Couple." He switched on the projector and brought up a black-and-white picture of a smiling couple on their wedding day.

Almost everyone recognized the young version of the oldest couple in their church, who'd been married nearly seventy years. An image of Queen Elizabeth and Prince Philip setting off on a ship as a young couple came next, followed by a comical wedding photo of a couple from the church married in the 1970s, when long hair and powder blue tuxedoes had been all the rage. After Will exhausted his collection of couple pictures, the church organist seated herself at the small piano beside him for a game of Name That Tune.

Mary played a variety of popular love songs, most being guessed correctly after a few notes. Sergeant Adam Oduba, an apparent music afficionado, won a box of chocolates, which he immediately gave to his wife, Merrilee. The two were adorable, sporting snazzy outfits each with tasteful purple accents. It was nice to see Seargeant Oduba outside of his official capacity.

Next came a version of the Newlywed Game, for which Will selected volunteer couples whose most recent anniversaries ranged from two years to forty. He asked a variety of questions, and the couples, with their backs to each other, wrote their answers on large cards. Then they would show their answers to see if they matched.

Watching the husbands deliberate over how their wives would answer Will's questions was comical, but listening to the wives' responses was even more so. It came as no surprise that the longest-married couple got the most correct answers, with the only missed question being the right way to hang a roll of toilet paper. Most of the women in the room were adamant that it should unroll from the top—a revelation to Harriet, who'd never given it a moment's thought. To think she'd been fretting over how she could possibly be a good wife and mother while running a thriving vet practice, utterly oblivious to the little things that could tear a couple apart, like hanging the toilet paper the wrong way. She had to chuckle at the idea.

But by far her favorite part of the game was the youngest couple's answer to "What's the most romantic thing your husband has done for you in the past week?" Everyone laughed when the guy responded, "I did the dishes." But laughter and applause burst forth when his wife had the same answer.

When Will handed off emcee duties for the next activity and joined Harriet at the table, he whispered to her, "I may have a house-keeper take care of the parsonage, but I always do my own dishes."

Harriet giggled, earning her curious glances from Elaine and Tamzin.

Karaoke serenading came next, some better than others. When Will pushed on the table to stand, Harriet grabbed his arm. "Don't you dare." If he planned to declare his love to her for the first time, she didn't want the romantic gesture to be in front of a roomful of his congregants.

He laughed. "No worries. I'm going to the kitchen to let them know they can start serving pudding."

She waved him on, adding in a proper British accent, "Good show. Carry on."

Tamzin leaned over after he walked away. "I don't know how you do it. I don't think I could stand being a minister's wife. Leading ladies' missionary meetings, visiting shut-ins all the time, always being scrutinized for what I'm doing or not doing. I'm surprised you'd be willing to give up your grandfather's veterinary practice."

Harriet was too shocked at Tamzin's comments to think before she spoke. "Who said anything about giving up my practice?"

Tamzin blinked. "Everyone knows a pastor's wife is expected to be his helpmate in the home and church."

"Perhaps once upon a time, Tamzin," Elaine interjected. "These days, no one expects a woman to give up her career when she gets married unless she wants to and the couple can afford it."

Harriet held up a hand. "We've only been dating a few weeks. We're a long way from—"

"Nonsense." Tamzin shook her head, her expression doting. "Anyone with two eyes can see the pastor is a goner for you. You're the first woman he's dated since he came here. And I certainly don't think he'd parade you in front of the entire congregation if his intentions weren't serious."

The butterflies swooped back into Harriet's stomach with a vengeance.

Elaine patted Harriet's hand on the table. "Stop scaring the poor lass, Tamzin."

Will returned to the table and frowned at her. "Are you okay? You've gone pale."

"Yes. Excuse me a minute." She rushed to the ladies' room, which was thankfully empty. Her stomach churned. This was exactly the kind of thing she'd feared. How could she live up to everyone's expectations of how a pastor's future wife should act? She didn't want to spend the rest of her life letting Will's congregation down.

She was a veterinarian, which meant sometimes she would miss a Sunday morning service or a Wednesday night small group meeting. It also meant she wouldn't be available to sit on every committee or accompany Will on all his visitations. If people couldn't live with that, if Will couldn't live with that...

She braced her hands on the counter and stared at her pale face in the mirror. "If Will couldn't live with that, then what?" What was she willing to give up to be with him? Would she have to choose between upholding her family's legacy in the career she'd built over years of hard work, and creating her own family with the man of her dreams—if Will was even the man for her?

Elaine came into the room and immediately met Harriet's gaze in the wall mirror.

Abruptly straightening, Harriet busied herself washing her hands.

As astute as her sister, Elaine wasn't fooled. "Don't pay any mind to Tamzin, dear. She means well. And considering we've had a bachelor pastor for some years now, I imagine everyone would carry on quite happily in their present roles and not expect to suddenly slough them off on a new bride."

"We've been on a few dates. That's all. It's too early to say whether it's serious."

Elaine patted Harriet's arm affectionately. "Don't you fret. When it's right, you'll know, and it won't matter what anyone else thinks. Even when it comes to a relationship with someone as public-spirited as Will is, the two of you have to work out what's best for you. It's no one else's business. The people who truly care about you merely want to see both of you happy, however that looks."

Harriet's heart quieted at the truth in the woman's words. "Thanks, Elaine."

Before Elaine could reply, Harriet's phone rang the special ringtone she'd assigned to Polly, who'd only be calling if they had an emergency.

"Sorry to interrupt your evening," Polly blurted when Harriet answered. "Ned Staveley at Goose Beck Farm is in a right state. He fears one of his Highland cows has staggers."

Harriet sucked in a breath. Although fairly rare, the magnesium deficiency known as staggers was an urgent veterinary emergency. "Tell him I'll come straightaway." Harriet ended the call and apologized to Elaine then returned to their table, her phone still in her hand. "I'm so sorry, Will, but I have to go. An emergency call's come in."

Will surged to his feet. "I'll come with you. You might need an extra pair of hands."

"Aren't you needed here?"

"My part is done, as long as Henry here is okay with locking up after the caterers have cleared out."

"Not a problem," Elaine's husband assured them.

Grinning, Will offered Harriet his hand. "I'm all yours."

Harriet's insides somersaulted, but the giddy feeling quickly dissipated at Tamzin's smirk.

"Nice eating with you," Harriet murmured to the table before heading off.

"Do you have a change of clothes with you?" Will asked as they hurried across the car park to the parsonage. "You could change inside. I wouldn't mind changing into something less nice myself."

"I appreciate the offer, but the sooner we go, the better chance the animal will have of surviving. Staggers has a quick progression time. If you don't start treatment within an hour or so, the cow could die."

Will's eyes widened. "Then we'd better get moving."

As she sped out of town a minute later, Will prayed aloud for safety on the road and for the sick cow.

Touched by his actions, Harriet murmured, "Thank you."

"I want to apologize for what happened back there," Will responded, catching her off guard. "Henry told me what Tamzin said when I left the table."

"That's not your fault."

"Nevertheless, I don't want you to feel you have to act a certain way because you're dating the pastor."

"I know. But not everyone feels the same way."

"I'm sure I could write a sermon to address that."

Harriet burst into laughter. "I'd be sitting in the pew, utterly mortified."

"Okay, that wouldn't do. Nix the sermon. But I want to nip this nonsense in the bud."

Harriet shifted gears for the steep incline, grateful for the distraction from what awaited them. "Tamzin said I'm the first woman you've dated since coming to White Church Bay. Is that true?"

"Yes. Before I came here I had a small church, back when I was young and eager and naive."

"Naive how?"

"I had no inkling of the kinds of ideas the older ladies were putting in the minds of the lasses I dated," Will explained.

"Perhaps they were trying to put them off so you'd consider their own daughters instead," Harriet teased.

"In one case, that was true. But it put me off dating altogether. I guess that's why I've favored quiet country walks and out-of-the-way restaurants for our dates. I don't want you to feel like you're in a fishbowl."

"I suspect I need to develop a thick skin so comments don't bother me. Tamzin didn't mean to be unkind. Her assumptions simply caught me by surprise."

"Well, if it happens again, please don't keep it to yourself. I don't want you to feel as if you're going through it alone."

"I appreciate that," she said, but doubted she'd feel comfortable tattling on an intrusive parishioner. They were nearing Goose Beck Farm, so Harriet pushed the concern from her mind and mentally prepared herself for the difficult task ahead.

When they arrived, Harriet snatched her bag from the boot and ran to the barn, grateful she always kept a magnesium injection ready to go for just such a scenario. Mr. Staveley was waiting inside with the cow.

"What are the symptoms, and when did you notice them?" Harriet asked as she dug through her bag for the magnesium.

"He's usually a very tame beast, but for the last half an hour or so, he's been aggressive. He's also grinding his teeth and can't seem to stand still," the farmer replied.

Harriet cast a practiced eye over the cow. "I agree. It's good that you called right away, Mr. Staveley. We're going to start with a supplemental injection. Please hold his head and talk to him. Will, I may need you to steady him while we do this."

The next few minutes were a flurry of activity while Harriet administered the injection and monitored the cow's response to it. As they did so, she asked Mr. Staveley about the contents of the feed he was using for his herd. He was a seasoned farmer so, as she'd expected, he had made sure his feed met his herd's nutritional requirements. She concluded that this specific animal must have simply missed some prime magnesium-rich bits of food.

To everyone's relief, the cow responded well to the supplement. As Harriet packed away her supplies and prepared a new magnesium injection for future use, she said, "Really good work spotting that so quickly, Mr. Staveley. Let's keep this guy separate from the herd for a little bit until he's got a few more meals in him. You can also add some supplements while he's recovering. If you want, I can take blood samples from the rest of the herd to make sure their levels are good. I'd rather make sure this was a fluke and not a bad batch of feed."

Mr. Staveley agreed at once. "Please do take the samples. You're not the type to want unnecessary testing."

Harriet's heart warmed at his trust in her. The farming community in White Church Bay hadn't been particularly easy to win over, but she seemed to be making progress with them at last. Harriet collected the blood samples and prepared to leave. "Lab results won't be in until next week, so in the meantime, I recommend supplementation for the whole herd to be safe."

"Aye, I'll do that. Thanks for everything, Doc."

Harriet and Will silently traversed the rolling hills back toward town at a more sedate speed. The adrenaline of the past hour had worn off, leaving both exhausted.

Will suddenly twisted in his seat. "Did you see that?"

Harriet eased off the gas. "See what?"

"Something between the trees reflected your headlights when we passed. It might be another vehicle." He met her gaze. "What if it's the sheep rustlers?"

CHAPTER FIFTEEN

Harriet pulled over to the side of the road and reached for her phone. "We should call the police."

Will stilled her hand. "Let's turn around first and confirm it is a vehicle. I don't want to call them out on a wild-goose chase if this is nothing."

"But if we spook them, there's no way Van will get here in time."

"That's true. You wait here, and I'll sneak back and take a peek." Will quietly slipped from the truck.

Harriet hurried out after him. "What if they're armed?"

"Why would they be armed to steal sheep in the middle of nowhere at night?" Will reasoned.

"Why are they stealing sheep in the first place?" Harriet shot back.

"Good point. We'll be extra careful."

To avoid being spotted in the moonlight, Harriet and Will crept down the road in the shadow of the hedgerow. Within seconds, they came upon a compact car parked behind some bushes near a farm gate. The door opened, and the driver slapped at the ceiling, extinguishing the interior light. But in the brief time the figure had been visible, a sickening recognition squeezed Harriet's chest.

"Right. That's all the proof I need." Will unlocked his phone, shielding the light from view with his hand. "I'm calling the police."

"No, wait," Harriet whispered, catching his arm. "This doesn't make sense."

"It's a hatchback. He could easily fit a sheep in the boot." Will began to dial.

Harriet clasped his hand to stop him. "It isn't a *he*. It's my intern, Dierdre. Please let me talk to her first." She tapped on her phone's flashlight and trotted toward Dierdre's car. "Dierdre, what's going on?"

"Harriet?" Surprise mingled with relief in Dierdre's voice. "You scared me half to death. I thought you were a sheep rustler."

Harriet peered into the car, checking the front and back seats. "Are you alone?"

"I am. What are you two doing here?"

"On our way home from a vet call. You?" Harriet crossed one jacket flap over the other and crossed her arms over the top of them to ward off the cold.

"Tristan and I have been taking turns watching for rustlers ever since Mr. Digger discovered some of his sheep missing yesterday morning. I was scared that Nana and Grandad's flock might be targeted next."

"This field belongs to your grandparents?" Will asked.

"They rent it from the owner. Tristan and I have been trying to figure out the best way to safeguard the flock. That's why I was late to the farmers association meeting last night."

Harriet tamped down a suspicion that Dierdre was feeding her a story. "Why didn't you tell me?" She had read somewhere that when people were lying, they felt the need to supply more information than they'd been asked for. But this was Dierdre. She was always talkative. And she had been bending over backward to help them find Prince Charming.

"The guy in front of us shushed us. Remember? And Reggie was already doing his presentation. By the time he was done, we got talking about other things."

Harriet exchanged a glance with Will as Polly's unnerving observation linking recent vet calls to the victimized farms replayed in her thoughts. She couldn't disagree with Dierdre's timeline, but with all the sheep-rustling talk last night, it seemed odd that she hadn't mentioned anything about taking precautions to protect her grandparents' sheep.

Then again, perhaps she would have mentioned it if they'd worked together today. Or if they hadn't found her lurking out here tonight, maybe she would have brought it up tomorrow. Besides, if Dierdre was knowingly feeding information to the thief, she'd presumably have no reason to fear her grandparents would be targeted.

But what about Tristan? Was he merely playing along with Dierdre's watchdog plan to make himself appear above suspicion? Or was he as unwitting a cog in the scheme as Dierdre might be?

"Do you plan to stay here by yourself all night?" Will asked Dierdre.

"No, Tris is relieving me at midnight." Dierdre shifted her focus to Harriet. "Don't worry. I'll be at the clinic at nine like I promised."

"There's got to be a better way to safeguard the sheep," Will said. "The thief probably won't even strike if he catches a glimpse of your car's reflectors like I did."

"That's good. I'm not keen to face them."

"I'm surprised your father didn't kibosh the idea for that reason alone." Concern vied with skepticism in Will's tone.

"He and Mum went away for the weekend. It's their anniversary."

"So they don't know what you're up to?"

Dierdre squirmed, remaining mute.

Will glanced at his watch. "I'm not comfortable leaving you here alone in the dark. You're not even within sight of a farmhouse. What would you have done if we'd been sheep rustlers?"

"Called the police and gotten your license number. Maybe slash your tires while you were in the pasture so you couldn't get far with whatever sheep you nicked."

Harriet chuckled. "Clever." She nudged Will. "What do you say we sit and wait until Tristan gets here?" It wasn't the romantic ending she'd pictured to their first Valentine's Day together, but after spending the last hour in a cow barn, she wasn't feeling terribly romantic anyway.

"You'd do that?" Dierdre's hopeful tone solidified Harriet's conviction that there was nothing suspicious about the girl's presence.

Harriet tilted her head to meet Will's gaze. "Are you okay with staying out a little later than we planned?"

"Sure."

They climbed into the back seat. "I thought you'd be spending the evening with Reggie," Harriet said, attempting to rub warmth into her hands. Will clasped them between his, warming her from the inside out.

Dierdre sighed, clearly frustrated. "With the start of lambing, Reggie doesn't want to be away from the farm."

"A few of the church's farming couples missed tonight's Valentine's party for the same reason," Will commiserated.

Dierdre shrugged and rummaged through a grocery sack beside her. "I could've kept him company at his place. But Tristan already had plans for this stakeout, and I'd have a hard time forgiving myself if I didn't help him protect Grandad's sheep."

Harriet wondered if the romance between Dierdre and Reggie was cooling now that his farm responsibilities were interfering with their social life. Harriet squeezed Will's hand, grateful he'd been more than willing to spend an evening with her hanging out in a barn.

Opening a bag of potato chips, Dierdre helped herself to a handful and then offered the bag to Harriet and Will. "Crisps?"

"No thanks." Confident that no rustlers would strike with two vehicles parked beside the pasture, Harriet took the opportunity to ask Dierdre a question that had been bothering her. "Have you and Tristan talked to his friend who drives the black van about the recent thefts?"

"I don't know about Tris, but I've never spoken more than a few words to Zee."

"Zee? That's his name?"

"I doubt it's what his parents named him, but it's what he goes by."

"How much do you know about him? What does he do for a living?"

Dierdre bit her bottom lip. "I don't know. I never asked."

Given her talkative nature, Harriet suspected Dierdre had said more to Zee than she might realize. And if Harriet didn't want Dierdre growing defensive of herself or her brother, she needed to tread carefully. She softened her tone. "Listen, this might come as a surprise, but Polly realized that all the recent disappearances were from farms where you and I had visited. And it occurred to me that with your enthusiasm for discussing what you've learned, you might've inadvertently tipped off the wrong person to some golden opportunities."

Even in the car's dim interior, Harriet didn't miss how Dierdre's face paled. "I never talked to Zee about our farm visits. Honest. I scarcely talk to him at all."

"I believe you," Harriet assured her. "What about with your family? Do you talk about our visits at the dinner table?"

Dierdre shrugged. "I guess."

"So Zee could've tapped Tristan for the information."

Dierdre's eyes widened, and she shook her head vigorously. "Tris wouldn't do that. Not ever. I thought the police were investigating that guy who stole the van."

"Actually, Simon Boyes didn't steal the van," Will said. "I spoke with him this afternoon."

Harriet cocked her head. "What happened?"

"The son of the couple who borrowed the van from the Galloways used it to drive his girlfriend to a house party in Whitby Sunday night when his parents were away for the weekend. But his girlfriend wound up flirting with another bloke, so he walked out on her, only to realize she had the keys in her purse."

"Simon told you this?" Harriet strained to keep the skepticism from her voice.

"No, Ian did. I went to the Abbott house to speak to Simon, but they told me he was working. Ian came home from school while I was there, so I asked him what they were really doing Sunday night before we saw them."

"And?" Harriet prodded.

"The boy who used the Galloways' van called Ian to pick him up from the party. Ian took his friends, including Simon, along for the ride. Once they got there, Simon suggested they mess with the girlfriend by moving the van. That way if she went out to drive it home, she'd find herself out of luck."

"How'd they move it when he didn't have the key?"

"The back hatch wasn't locked, so one of them climbed in and shifted it into neutral then steered while the rest of the lads pushed it around the corner."

"Was that why they acted so cagey when you asked them what they'd been up to?" Harriet asked.

"I suspect so. But the joke ended up being on the boy, because by the time the girlfriend returned the keys and he caught a lift back to Whitby to retrieve the van, the police had already impounded it."

"Did you share all this with Van?" Harriet asked.

"Aye. He spoke to the boy's parents, and the last I heard he was planning to question all the lads who were involved."

Dierdre crumpled the empty bag and stuffed it into the grocery sack. "So you don't think the abandoned van has anything to do with the sheep rustling?"

"If Ian's version of the story is true, then it appears not."

Dierdre shifted so she was sitting sideways with her feet in the passenger seat. "Which makes Zee sound like a better suspect. He's got a van too."

"If he *is* our sheep rustler, Tristan might not have realized how Zee's been using him."

Dierdre frowned. "I'll ask Tris what he and Zee talk about. They have been spending a lot of time together. I suppose that means there's a chance Tris might have repeated some of my stories to him." She blinked rapidly. "I'm so sorry. I know I talk too much."

"This isn't your fault," Harriet told her. "You love to learn, and there's nothing wrong with that. You aren't responsible if someone decides to do bad things based on what they heard from you."

"And we don't want you confronting Zee or even tipping off your brother to these suspicions without any proof," Will added. "If the opportunity arises, perhaps you could casually ask Tristan if he's ever shared your farm stories with anyone. And perhaps what Zee does for a living."

"It would be helpful too," Harriet ventured, "if you could sneak into his van and search for any evidence he's transported animals in there. But only if there's absolutely no chance he could catch you."

Dierdre plunked her feet back to the floorboards and straightened. "I can do that."

"But like Will said, don't mention our suspicions, even to your brother," Harriet cautioned. "Because if Tristan can't believe his friend would use him that way, he might gripe to Zee before the police get a chance to get any evidence against him."

"*If* he's even guilty," Will amended.

"Of course," Harriet agreed. She admired how Will always chose to believe the best about people. Unlike her, who seemed to be swept away easily by the suspicions of others.

"I'll be careful what I say. I'll make up an excuse for why I'm in his van," Dierdre said. "You can count on me. I'll make this right."

Harriet's heart clenched at the girl's anguish. "That implies you did something wrong, Dierdre. You didn't."

Dierdre nodded, but her expression said she wasn't convinced.

The rest of the evening crawled by, with Dierdre checking her watch every five minutes. "I don't know what could be keeping Tris.

He's usually so punctual." At five past midnight, she tried calling him. "He's not picking up."

"Hopefully because he's on his way," Harriet said encouragingly.

Just then, Harriet's phone rang. She sucked in a breath at the sight of Aunt Jinny's name on her screen then answered. "Aunt Jinny, is everything okay?"

Her aunt's voice held a note of concern. "Can you come home right away?"

CHAPTER SIXTEEN

Harriet tugged on Will's sleeve to let him know something was up. "What's going on?"

"A man found four kittens abandoned on the side of the road and brought them here. He said he didn't know how to help them himself but he hoped you would. When you didn't answer at the clinic or at the main house, he came and knocked on my door. I figured you were out on an emergency call if you weren't still on your date with Will."

"How old are the kittens?" Harriet asked.

"I'm not sure, but they can't be very old. Their eyes aren't even open yet."

"And no mother, I'm assuming?"

"He searched but didn't find one. He thought with as young as they seem to be that a mother wouldn't voluntarily have left them for very long."

"That's probably true," Harriet agreed. "Okay, I'm on my way." She hung up and quickly filled in Will and Dierdre. "I'll need to get them to the clinic where we can keep them warm. Unless you know of a mother cat who recently had kittens and would adopt a few more, they'll probably have to be fed every couple of hours."

"I can do it," Dierdre said.

"What about school?"

"It's half-term break, remember?" Dierdre pointed out. "Please. It feels like I'm meant to help them. If we hadn't run into each other, or if Tristan had been on time, I wouldn't even know about them."

"Okay, but we can't afford to wait around for your brother now," Harriet said. "The sooner we start caring for the kittens, the better their chances of survival. I have enough supplement at the clinic to see them through the weekend. We can order more."

Dierdre nodded. "I'll text Tristan to let him know and then follow you to Cobble Hill. Do you think Polly will mind if I leave them with her at the clinic when I go with you on calls tomorrow and next week?"

"I'm sure she'll be delighted," Harriet answered.

"I can pop in and lend her a hand if she needs one," Will volunteered.

"That's good of you. Between all of us, we'll make it work. Let's get to it."

Harriet and Will hurried to the Land Rover then sped back to the clinic.

"What are the chances we can keep them alive?" Will asked.

Harriet's grip tightened on the steering wheel. "I'm not sure yet. It'll depend on what kind of shape they're in, which will be affected by how old they are and how long they've been on their own. They might not be able to regulate their temperature yet, so we'll need to see they're kept warm—but not too warm. And we'll need to feed them as soon as we can."

"I'll help however I can," Will promised. "I might need some training though. I've never rescued abandoned kittens before."

She shot him a quick smile. "I appreciate it, and I'm sure you'll be as great with this as you were with our bovine patient earlier this evening."

"I think you're just saying that," he accused, clearly trying to lighten the mood.

"No, really. I think you have a gift," she insisted. "Animals can often sense human emotions, so someone as calm and even-keeled as you tends to put them at ease. I truly think I would have had much more trouble with that injection if you hadn't been there to steady the cow."

"I'm glad to know I was useful," Will said.

"Very." She grimaced. "I'm sorry my job spoiled your plans for the evening."

"Is that what you think?"

"It's been one emergency after another," she lamented. "We had to leave early from the lovely dinner you probably worked really hard to put together. I wouldn't blame you for being annoyed about it."

Will laid his hand over hers on the gearshift. "Harriet, my plan for the evening was to spend it with you, and that's exactly what I'm doing. I really couldn't care less what that entails, but helping you save animals who need you is much better than anything I could have come up with."

His words pushed away some of her discomfort from what Tamzin had said at dinner. "If you're sure."

"I'm positive."

As they made the rest of the drive to the clinic, Harriet went over instructions for the kittens and Will took her directions in his usual imperturbable manner. Back at Cobble Hill Farm, Harriet,

Will, and Dierdre retrieved the kittens from the dower cottage, with Harriet assuring the man who'd brought them that he'd done the right thing. Then the three of them hurried the cardboard box of tiny gray kittens to the clinic.

After Dierdre headed home with the kittens fed and snuggled up to a hot water bottle, Harriet drove Will to the parsonage.

"Thanks for everything, Will. I really appreciate all you've done tonight."

He smiled at her. "I was happy to help. You should get some rest, at least as long as you're between emergency calls."

"You too. Thank you for the lovely evening. And the flowers."

"Thank you for the card and the adventures." He hesitated, and for a brief moment, she wondered if he would kiss her under the moonlight. But instead, he wrapped his arms around her, squeezed, and then stepped back. "I'll call you later, okay?"

"Okay. Good night."

As she drove home, Harriet couldn't decide whether she was disappointed or relieved that they hadn't had their first kiss in the wee hours of the morning after an adrenaline-filled night.

Harriet woke Saturday morning to a pounding on her bedroom door.

"Harriet? Are you okay?" Polly called. "Your first appointment is in ten minutes."

Harriet's eyes sprang open, and she leaped out of bed. "I'll be there in a few minutes. Sorry, I had a late night dealing with orphaned kittens and must've forgotten to plug my phone in the charger."

She scanned the bedside table as she changed, but her phone wasn't there.

"You left it on my desk in the clinic. I've plugged it in the charger over there. And Dierdre called to say she'll be another half hour yet because she wants to feed the kittens one more time before she comes in."

"Sounds good." Harriet pulled her hair into a ponytail.

"Would you like me to make you something for breakfast?" Polly asked.

"That's okay. I'll grab a breakfast bar. But—"

"Coffee's already made," Polly said with a chuckle, apparently reading Harriet's mind. "See you downstairs."

At the sound of Polly's fading footsteps, Harriet hurried to the bathroom to wash up and brush her teeth. She was glad she'd taken the extra few minutes to shower the previous night before she'd fallen into bed. And that was another reason to be grateful Will hadn't tried to kiss her. The hours she kept were enough of a relationship challenge without his memories of their first kiss being tied to the smell of a cow barn in her hair.

Harriet managed to down a protein bar and a cup of coffee before their first client of the morning arrived. When she emerged from the exam room twenty minutes later, Van was chatting with Polly at the reception desk. And for once, Polly wasn't frenziedly trying to climb out of her skin to avoid being in the same room with him.

In fact, she was smiling and appeared completely at ease.

Maybe there was hope yet for a happy ending for the pair.

Harriet returned the file to Polly as their client paid for the visit.

Stepping aside, Van nodded. "Nice catching up with you, Polly."

"Did you bring news for us?" Harriet asked when his attention finally shifted her way.

"I did."

The only person in the waiting room was an older woman with no pet in sight. Harriet lifted a finger. "One second, please. Polly, who's our next client?"

"Rover, to get his cast off. But he's not due for ten minutes."

That didn't explain who the woman was, but hopefully that would become clear with time. "Okay. Van, what can I do for you?"

He motioned to the woman to join them. She rose slowly, the grimace crossing her face suggesting she suffered from achy joints.

"Harriet," Van said, "this is my neighbor, Vivien Smith."

"Hello," Harriet replied, nonplussed. Why had Van brought his neighbor to her clinic?

"It's good to meet you, Dr. Bailey. I'll get right to it. I used to run a cat rescue in this area before I retired a few years ago. This morning, my grandson came to visit me—he checks on me a couple of times a week, you see—and mentioned that he'd brought some kittens to you last night. He knows I still like to hear about things like that, and I'd taught him some basic rescue things, like searching for a mother cat to make sure the kittens have actually been abandoned and such."

"You taught him well. I'm glad he found them when he did and brought them to us."

"He probably would have brought them to me, but he thinks I do too much as it is," Mrs. Smith said with a chuckle. "I asked dear Van to bring me to you so I can offer my help in another way. I still have contacts from my rescuing days. I'd be happy to tap them for donations to pay for the kittens' care until they're ready for permanent homes. I'd also love to find those forever homes for them. In fact, I'd like to keep one of the kittens myself. My own cat passed away a few months ago of old age, and I'm tired of rattling around my home all by myself."

Harriet didn't think she'd ever get used to White Church Bay. Just when she thought she'd reached the extent of its residents' kindness and generosity, they found a new way to surprise her. "That's wonderful. Thank you so much, Mrs. Smith."

"Vivien," she corrected firmly. "Is it okay with you if I see the kittens?"

"Of course," Harriet replied. "If you have time to wait. Our intern, who will be responsible for the bulk of their care, took them home last night and should be in soon."

Viven clapped her hands together with a gleeful expression. "Smashing. As long as Van here doesn't mind."

"Not at all," Van assured her. "I went off duty an hour ago."

"It's so nice of you to bring Vivien here on your own time." Harriet smothered a smile, knowing he likely welcomed having a legitimate excuse to see Polly.

His answering grin told her that was exactly what he'd been thinking.

"Any new developments in the sheep-rustling cases?" Harriet asked as Vivien settled back in her chair. "Will told me the stolen van wasn't exactly stolen."

"That's right. The Galloways aren't pressing charges or anything."

"You believe the boy's story?"

"His would-be date for the evening confirmed that they got to the party in Whitby at seven. So if he pinched the Danbys' tup when you heard an engine here, it wouldn't have given him much time to offload it and change before picking her up."

"That's true," Harriet admitted.

"Since we don't have exact times for the previous thefts, it's tough to confirm his alibis. But he hasn't had a vehicle at his disposal since Sunday, so I doubt he's connected to the incidents since then."

Rover's owner held the front door for Dierdre, who carried in the box of kittens. "Good morning, Harriet," she chirped, as bright-eyed as ever in spite of the minimal sleep she must have gotten the night before. "What should I do with these little ones?"

"Let's take them to my office. Vivien, feel free to join us to meet the kittens." Harriet smiled at her next patient. "I'll be right with you."

Vivien excitedly followed Harriet and Dierdre to the office.

"Any trouble getting them to eat?" Harriet asked Dierdre.

"Not a bit. I think they're stronger already."

"Great." Harriet made introductions then drew the drapes and dimmed the lights. "The kittens can stay in here for now. It's best to keep them in dim light and away from drafts. Take all the time you need to introduce Vivien to the kittens. Then, when you're free, you can join me in the exam room."

"Will do," Dierdre said.

Returning to reception, Harriet nodded to Betty, Rover's owner, and collected the collie's file. Meanwhile, Van reclaimed his earlier post at the reception desk and quietly waited for Polly to finish her call.

"Actually, DC Worthington, who's working on several similar incidents, is here. I'll pass you over to him." Polly muffled the receiver with her hand. "Felicity Barnes is on the line. Someone's nicked Bo Peep, her blue-ribbon Hampshire Down gimmer." Polly handed him the phone. "The poor woman is a mess."

Harriet's heart sank. "I'm sorry," she said to Betty. "Could you take Rover to the exam room? I'll be there in just a minute."

"No rush, love. Take your time. Rover and I have nowhere we need to be."

Harriet nodded her thanks then read the notes Van was scribbling onto his notepad. Based on what she could decipher, Bo Peep had gone missing the night before from the pasture behind the barn.

The instant Van finished on the phone, Harriet blurted, "Simon Boyes was working at Felicity's, mending fences. How sure are you that the story he spun about the stolen van isn't something he concocted with his friends after the fact? I saw him with a wad of cash the day after Prince Charming went missing. And now a sheep has gone missing from a farm he had inside knowledge about."

"I'll ask him where he was last night."

"And ask the other victims if Simon worked for them. If you haven't already, that is." Harriet was probably telling Van things he already knew, but if she didn't say them, she was worried they would somehow be missed. "I know you're supposed to be off, but any livestock auctions open today must be notified immediately, or you might miss your chance to catch someone trying to sell Bo Peep."

"I'll take care of it. I promise," Van assured her. "Thank you, Harriet."

Harriet nodded. She supposed Van, as a detective constable, was subject to the same kind of unpredictable demands on his time as she was. "Thank you. I'm sorry. I know you're working above and beyond on this." She hitched her thumb toward the exam room. "And I need to get back to work myself."

But as Harriet walked to the exam room, the soft strains of Dierdre's chattering with Vivien in her office stirred another thought. Tristan hadn't shown up to take over watching his grandparents' flock last night—a day after likely hearing Dierdre's tales of Felicity's blue-ribbon ewe. Nor had he answered his phone when Dierdre called him.

Suddenly Harriet had to wonder what Tristan was up to when Bo Peep disappeared.

CHAPTER SEVENTEEN

Harriet struggled to keep her mind on removing Rover's cast as she tried to determine the best way to ask Dierdre about her brother's whereabouts last night. Although Dierdre clearly wanted the sheep rustler caught, she might not prove particularly helpful if she thought Harriet suspected Tristan.

"…activities?" Rover's owner's voice penetrated Harriet's thoughts.

"I'm sorry." Harriet held a steadying hand on the collie on the exam table and shifted her focus to his owner. "What was your question? I'm afraid you caught me with my mind wandering."

Betty smiled kindly. "I understand. I asked if Rover could resume his normal activities."

"Oh, yes. The leg has healed beautifully. It shouldn't give him any more trouble."

"Grand." Betty lifted the dog to the floor. "It's time we have a proper walk again, isn't it, boy?" She left to settle her bill with Polly.

Dierdre slipped into the room as Harriet disinfected the examination table. "Would you like me to call in the next patient?"

Harriet tossed the disinfecting wipe in the rubbish bin and took a fresh one to clean the counter. "We have a few minutes yet. How are the kittens taking to the bottle?"

"Super. They're greedy little mites. Tris said he would see if he could rig up something that would allow the lot of them to feed at once. He loves inventing things."

Harriet latched on to the perfect segue. "Did he say why he didn't show up for guard duty last night?"

"Yeah. The car he was borrowing from a mate got a flat, and there was no spare in the boot. His date called her father, who came and fetched her, but left Tris behind to deal with the car."

"Without a spare?"

Dierdre shrugged. "He probably assumed Tris would call a breakdown van, but a tow is the last thing he wants to spend money on right now."

"What did he do?" Harriet washed the counter a second time, wanting to get the whole story before bringing in their next client.

"He called Zee. They eventually sorted it and returned the car to his mate. Zee dropped Tris at our house when they didn't find me with the flock. Then Tris drove my car to the pasture to keep watch the rest of the night."

"You must be exhausted," Harriet said. "I was dead to the world until Polly hammered on my door this morning." She tossed the second wipe then washed her hands. "It's a shame Tristan didn't answer his phone last night. We could've taken him the spare from your car to get him on the road again."

"I never asked him why he didn't answer my calls or text to tell me he'd be late. You know how guys are. They never think about things like that."

"I imagine he was frazzled and perhaps didn't hear the phone ring."

"Or he had the ringer off so it wouldn't interrupt his date," Dierdre suggested.

"That would've been considerate of him." Harriet attempted to sound positive as she searched Dierdre's face for any indication she doubted her brother's story.

Dierdre ducked her head. "Is it horrible of me to be grateful that the Barneses' flock was targeted last night instead of my grandfather's?"

"Of course not. But it is surprising, isn't it?"

"How do you mean?"

"Felicity's pasture doesn't flank a road," Harriet reminded her. "In fact, the fold Bo Peep was in isn't even visible from the road."

Dierdre's eyes widened. "Which means the thief had to know about the ewe and where it was kept ahead of time. That's why you figured it had to be Simon."

"Yes. Unless…" Harriet drew in a deep breath, still nervous about Dierdre's reaction if she hinted that Tristan might in any way be connected to Bo Peep's disappearance.

Dierdre must have guessed what Harriet was thinking—or something similar anyway—because she blurted, "You think it might've been Zee." She cupped her hand over her mouth.

Harriet waited for an explanation for her reaction.

Dierdre shook her head. "I'm so sorry. That probably sounds crazy."

"No crazier than some of my theories. What made you say it though?" Harriet prodded. "Did you talk about Felicity's sheep with Zee?"

"Not with Zee, no. But I went on and on about how cute Bo Peep is to Tris. I told him that if he started his own flock one day he should think about getting into more valuable specialty breeds. Not that Hampshire Downs are all that rare. But some of the rarer breeds fetch much more at auction."

"You might be onto something there." Harriet tilted her head as a new thought struck her.

"What are you thinking?"

"I've assumed our thief has been stealing for a quick profit, especially after I saw Simon flashing all that cash. But what if that's not it at all? Maybe he hasn't targeted easier-to-access livestock, because he's filling a shopping list. It would explain why he'd risk venturing onto the Barnes property to snatch Bo Peep."

"A shopping list?" Dierdre echoed, puzzled.

"Yeah, like you said, a specialty breeder has a better chance of turning a profit these days. And all the better chance if he acquires prizewinning ewes and champion sires at no cost to him."

Dierdre shook her head. "But the Danbys' tup was a regular old Suffolk, champion or not. Any lambs he sired wouldn't be rare breeds and wouldn't fetch the same value."

Harriet deflated. "True. We've got to be missing something."

"I think so," Dierdre agreed. "If the stolen sheep were being sold at auction, you'd think the detectives would've gotten a whiff of a dodgy exchange or two by now."

"Good point." Harriet glanced at the time. "We'd better see to our next patient."

Dierdre exited the room and then escorted an Old English sheepdog and his owner to the room for an annual checkup.

Shortly after Dierdre left to give the kittens their next feeding, Will entered the waiting room. "I've come to see how our rescues are doing."

"I'll go give Dierdre a hand with the feeding if that's okay," Polly said to Harriet. "We don't have any other appointments scheduled for today, and I can monitor the phones from the line in your office."

"That's great. Thanks," Harriet agreed, certain Polly's reason for making herself scarce had as much to do with giving Harriet time alone with Will as with a burning desire to help feed adorable kittens.

Will grinned. "Sounds as if everyone is eager for a chance to play surrogate mother."

Harriet motioned to the teapot being kept warm in a knitted cozy. "Would you like a cup of tea?"

"I'd love one."

Since the clinic was still technically open to walk-in clients for the next half hour, Harriet suggested they enjoy their tea in a corner of the waiting room in case anyone came in. Then she filled Will in on Vivien's generosity.

"That's great." Will beamed, obviously proud of the village he called home. "All's well that ends well, right?"

"The night didn't end so well for the Barneses." Harriet told him about the theft and her discussion with Dierdre, omitting her earlier—and lingering—suspicions of Simon Boyes.

"Have you told Van your theory that the thief might be targeting specific breeds?"

"Not yet," Harriet admitted. "And given Tristan's going AWOL on Dierdre last night and her inability to get him on the phone, I'm not ready to dismiss him as a suspect." Harriet glanced at her closed office door and lowered her voice. "But I didn't want to mention those suspicions to Van in front of her."

Will sighed. "I imagine he or one of his superiors will want to speak to Simon again too, given that he worked for Felicity."

Harriet sipped her tea. "It is an uncomfortable coincidence."

"Only because of his past. Like you said, you've been to each farm that's been targeted within days of the thefts. The only reason that doesn't seem coincidental is because no one could imagine you having a motive to steal their sheep."

"Sure, but how long before the farmers make the connection between Dierdre's presence with me and the possibility that she has an ulterior motive for all those questions she asks?"

Will nearly dropped his teacup and gaped at Harriet. "You don't believe that. Do you?"

"No, of course not. But others don't know her the way I do."

"Do you have any farm calls after lunch?" Will asked.

"No. But I'm determined to get to the bottom of this sheep rustling, and I intend to start by paying Felicity a visit. Maybe see if she noticed any strange vehicles lurking in the area yesterday or saw any tracks this morning."

"I was thinking the same thing. Although I'm sure the detectives have asked those questions, so perhaps our time might be better spent trailing Dierdre's brother and his friend Zee. I drove past the pasture Dierdre was staking out last night, thinking her brother might be on guard duty, but no one was about."

"He does contract milking."

"And I imagine the risk of theft isn't as high come daylight."

"And presumably if Zee is using Tristan to gain inside information, he wouldn't target Tristan's own family. Do you think it's terrible of me to suspect someone I don't even know?"

Will squeezed her hand. "You're considering suspects who have motive, means, and opportunity. And although we don't know Zee's financial situation, money tends to be a strong motive regardless. His van gives him the means."

"And I'm assuming the fact that he met Tristan at a sheep-herding trial means he spends a lot of time around sheep and probably knows of several such farms locally," Harriet mused.

"Sounds like a reasonable assumption. But what we don't know is whether Tristan has been feeding him information about the flocks that you and Dierdre have visited."

"Correct." Harriet collected their empty cups to wash later.

Will rose and approached the desk. "I assume Dierdre hasn't had the chance to broach the subject with him yet?"

"Broach what subject?" Dierdre strode into the waiting room with Polly.

Harriet jumped, which probably made her appear incredibly guilty. She cleared her throat. "We wondered if you asked Tristan if he ever talked with Zee about our farm visits."

"Oh. No, sorry. I was kind of preoccupied with the kittens this morning."

Will grinned at Harriet. "Do you mind if I sneak back to the office and take a peek at them?"

"Go right ahead."

Dierdre watched Will disappear through the office door. "I'll ask Tristan the next time I see him. I promise. As long as Zee isn't around anyway."

"I appreciate that."

Dierdre nervously nibbled on her thumbnail.

"Did you think of something else that might be pertinent?" Polly probed.

Dierdre lowered her hand. "Maybe. You know I talk a lot, right?"

"It's okay, Dierdre," Harriet assured her. "The farmers we visit happily answer your questions."

"I know Doreen was chuffed about your curiosity regarding their farming operation," Polly added. "I'm sure the other farmers are too."

"Maybe. But I'm sure they didn't think I'd babble what they shared to anyone who'd listen."

Polly chuckled. "You're generous about sharing your knowledge. I'm sure most of them would understand that. And in the Danbys' case, you were helping them by spreading word of mouth about their farm tours."

Dierdre's cheeks reddened. "My gran always warned me that curiosity killed the cat."

"Enough of that," Harriet said firmly. "You haven't done anything wrong, as I believe we've already discussed. Asking questions and then explaining the answers to others is how you learn, and your passion for learning is admirable. You are not responsible for what others do with the knowledge you share."

Polly shut down the office computer and gathered her coat. "On that note, our day's finished, and I need to head out. I'll see you Monday." To Harriet, she added, "And I'll see you at church."

"Do we have any farm calls this afternoon?" Dierdre asked.

"No. The rest of the day is clear," Harriet said. "We'll see you Monday."

"I'll be here." Dierdre hitched her thumb toward the office. "Should I take the kittens now?"

"Of course." Harriet walked the teen to her office where they found Will cuddling a kitten against his broad chest as he studied the map on her desk.

Will tapped some of the spots she'd marked on the map. "Are these the locations of the thefts?"

"That's right."

"I didn't realize what a large area your practice covers."

"It actually extends a fair way farther south than this too." Harriet dug a mathematics compass out of the desk drawer and poked the point into the location of Cobble Hill Farm then drew a wide circle. "The circle represents everything that's within about an hour's drive. My grandfather decided any place farther than that couldn't be accessed in a timely enough fashion to properly serve them. I occasionally stretch outside that range, particularly if a farmer's regular vet isn't available."

Will tilted his head, still studying the map, then gingerly returned the kitten to its box before extending his open palm toward her. "Can I see that compass for a minute?" He narrowed the angle of the legs then drew a circle that neatly enclosed all the farms that had reported sheep missing. "I don't know if it means anything, but it seems to me that all the thefts have occurred within half an hour of this point."

Dierdre squinted at the map and sucked in a breath. The next instant, she spun around and scooped up the box of kittens. "I'd better get going so I can eat lunch before I need to feed these little ones again."

"Are you sure you're okay to manage them all weekend?" Harriet asked.

"Uh, yeah. Sure." Dierdre sidled toward the door, clutching the box to her chest. "My friends will love to help with them."

Will nudged Harriet's arm as Dierdre left. "I think I'd like to adopt one of the kittens when they're old enough."

"Huh?" Harriet murmured, staring after the girl. "Oh, yes. That'd be great. You'll make a wonderful pet parent." She returned her attention to the map.

"What's wrong?" Will prodded.

"Didn't you notice?" Harriet grimaced, not liking where her thoughts had veered. "Dierdre saw something on this map. And given the way she hightailed it out of here, it freaked her out. We need to find out what that was about."

CHAPTER EIGHTEEN

Harriet tapped the center point of Will's circle on the map. "It's the Kingsbury Estate, where Dierdre and I went to see Samuel Bishop's journals for my article."

"Did she act strange while you were there?" Will asked.

"Not at all. So why is she suddenly jumpy about the possibility that it's at the center of the thefts?"

"Does her brother do contract work for them?"

"Not that she's mentioned." Another possibility came to mind. Harriet grabbed a pen and scribbled down the breeds and genders of the missing sheep.

"What are you doing?"

"One second." Harriet rummaged through the reference file she'd put together for her magazine article. Finding the page of decoded breeds, she laid it on the desk beside the list she'd just made. "What do you notice about the sheep from Samuel's journals and the missing sheep?"

Will studied the papers for a moment and then said, "The missing sheep are all on Samuel's list."

"Exactly. And perhaps more importantly, nothing was taken that isn't on his list, even though several of these farmers have more valuable breeds." Harriet pressed her fingertips to her mouth. Was it an uncanny coincidence? She highly doubted it.

"What are you thinking?" Will prodded.

"I think someone is attempting to recreate Samuel's breeding program. Whoever's behind the thefts is after early twentieth-century British breeds. And given that Samuel's journals are housed at the center of this circle, my guess is that it's one of Kingsbury's tenant farmers."

"Wow."

Excitement rose in Harriet's chest. "And now that I think about it, the woman at the livestock auction said someone had been in a few months ago, going through old invoice records to compile a breeding history. That can't be a coincidence, can it?"

"Did she say they were checking Samuel's records specifically?" Will sounded skeptical.

"She didn't specify. I didn't ask because it didn't seem relevant at the time. But the receptionist at the livestock auction might be able to identify our thief."

"It's a long shot. Even if the person was searching Samuel's records, he could've been a lackey of whoever's behind the scheme."

"Either way, it would be a connection. We have to follow every lead." Before she could second-guess herself, Harriet called the livestock auction office. Three rings later, voice mail picked up, inviting her to leave a message. She groaned. "They're already closed and don't open again until Wednesday. Maybe Van can get the name and personal number of the receptionist."

"We could pay a visit to the Kingsbury Estate and see if anyone has been there asking to see Samuel's journals," Will suggested. "Besides you, of course."

"Excellent idea. It had to be someone who was able to decipher the shorthand."

Will frowned. "On second thought, if someone at the estate is behind the scheme, then asking about the journals might not be smart. You never know how far a criminal will go to avoid being caught."

Harriet deflated. "This is the best lead we have right now. We can't abandon it." Studying the map, she tapped the trailhead of a public path that traversed the estate. "We could stroll along here. Maybe we'll spot where the stolen sheep have been squirreled away in plain sight."

Will's gaze shifted from the two lists to the map then to the lists again. "We should give what we've found to Van."

"You know as well as I do this isn't enough for him to secure a search warrant. And if the thief has kept the sheep close at hand, he won't for long after a DC shows up asking questions."

Will raised an eyebrow. "Giving Van the perfect opportunity to catch them."

Harriet stifled a frustrated huff. "How about we at least have an afternoon hike across the estate? It's a public path after all."

"So no one will suspect why we're really there?" Amusement colored Will's voice.

"Exactly. And if we happen to come across a talkative farmhand, we might be able to glean other information. Maybe you could ask if they need laborers because you know of one who's looking for work."

Will's brow furrowed. "I do?"

"Simon Boyes."

"Oh, yes. That's true."

"If we can get someone to drop the names of the tenant farmers there, we might find more connections."

Will raised an eyebrow at her. "When you start talking like that, I get nervous. I don't want to paint a target on your back."

"We'll be fine." Harriet folded the map. "But maybe wear your clerical collar. No one will suspect a minister of snooping."

Will gazed into her eyes, gently sweeping a wayward lock of hair from her face. His hazel eyes seemed darker than she remembered, almost brown. "Careful, Harriet Bailey. Someone might get the notion you're corrupting me."

Before she realized what she was doing, she moistened her lips. She could think of worse places for their first kiss than her beloved clinic. "I wouldn't want to do that," she whispered.

His responding grin crinkled the corners of his twinkling eyes. But instead of kissing her, he captured her hand in his. "Come on. I'll take you for lunch before we go on this sleuthing adventure of yours."

"Awesome. Let me change first."

Will escorted her into a dimly lit Tudor-style pub in a nearby hamlet. The mahogany-paneled walls were adorned with pastoral paintings of the moors. He chose seats by the leaded-pane windows overlooking the street.

With a promise to be right back, a server dropped menus of standard pub fare on the scarred, wooden table shellacked to a high sheen. When she returned, they ordered tomato soup and Cornish pasties. After filling their water glasses, the server left them to themselves.

"This is quaint." Harriet resisted the temptation to tease him about choosing places where they wouldn't be recognized. He did, after all, take her to the church dinner. And remembering Tamzin's needling about how a pastor's spouse should act, Harriet decided she quite preferred this. She shuddered.

"Are you cold?" Will shifted his chair closer and enclosed her hand in his warm one.

"I was thinking about Tamzin's comment last night."

Will groaned. "I'm sorry about that. I believe her insecurities give rise to some nervous chatter."

"Because of her embarrassment over dognapping Gwen Higginbottom's Scottish terrier a few months ago?"

"That's my guess."

"I'd noticed a bit of a change in how she interacts with me since that happened. Before, she'd never struck me as insecure." But as a pastor, Will might be privy to more going on in the woman's life than Harriet was aware of.

"You'd be surprised how many people exhibit either a gruff demeanor or an excessively flattering or agreeable air to avoid being hurt or rejected."

Recognizing how that could be a person's defense mechanism, Harriet squirmed in her seat. "I'm afraid I've discovered this past week that I can be too quick to judge. Like I did with one of my neighbors, I mean."

"It isn't always easy to discern whether a person's words and actions are merely pretense."

"Like the verse from your sermon last week. 'Watch out for false prophets. They come to you in sheep's clothing, but inwardly they are ferocious wolves.'"

"Yes, but you left out the most important part. 'You will recognize them by their fruit.'"

"But how can we? Couldn't that sometimes be pretense too?" Harriet wrung her hands. "I don't *want* to believe Tristan is knowingly conspiring with his friend to steal sheep, but what if all his help with the search is a calculated act to shift suspicion from himself?"

"I think this sleuthing might be making you a little cynical."

Harriet expelled a frustrated sigh. "I don't want to be. In fact, if Tristan wasn't chumming around with the likes of Zee, I don't think he would've made my suspect list at all. But after his not answering Dierdre's calls last night when Bo Peep disappeared, I'm not as inclined to cross him from the suspect list. And that was before Dierdre's suspicious reaction to the map."

"Tristan gleans the targets from Dierdre's tales of her farm visits, and Zee supplies the transportation. It's a reasonable theory," Will admitted. "No one would think it odd to see Tristan rambling about the countryside with his dog."

"Maybe Zee even befriended Tristan precisely to conscript him into working the scheme," Harriet said.

"But you think they're filling a shopping list for whoever's running the show out of the Kingsbury Estate?"

Harriet sighed, gripped by a wave of uncertainty. "Or maybe Simon Boyes is." She shrugged, knowing Will didn't want to believe it was Simon.

Will grimaced. "The more I think about this, the more convinced I am that the police should put the estate, the suspects, or both under surveillance."

"I have a better idea." She pulled the two lists from her purse and tapped on the breed from the journal that hadn't yet been reported stolen. "Whoever is filling this shopping list still needs a Lonk, one of the black-faced hill breeds. We might be able to use that."

"How?" Will asked.

"If I find a farm with Lonks, I could arrange to take Dierdre to it for the new wellness checks the government is paying for. Then we wait for our thief to make his move. Van can set up surveillance there."

Will sipped his water. "Would you tell Dierdre about the sting?"

"I don't think so. I don't think she's in cahoots with them, despite her suspicious reaction to the map. But she'd naturally want to protect her brother and might say more than she should."

Will's gaze darted about the room, then he leaned closer to Harriet and lowered his voice. "Assuming Dierdre's completely innocent, she already thinks her chattering tipped them off, so don't you think she'll stay mum about her farm visits from now on?"

Harriet groaned. "You might be right."

"On the other hand, her caring for those kittens gives us a good excuse to stop by. Maybe to offer to give her a break for an evening. We'll choose a time when Tristan is there and start chatting about the Lonks ourselves. That way we'll also be able to monitor his reaction."

"That's a very good idea." A text alert sounded on her phone, and Harriet read the message. "It's Dierdre. She's gotten answers to a few of our questions. Last night, Tristan was at a party until eleven. He blew the tire in his friend's car while driving his date home. The girl's father picked her up at eleven thirty. The rest of the time was spent dealing with the tire. But Tristan didn't arrive home until after two."

Will tapped his fingers on the table. "Two and a half hours is a long time to change a tire."

"Yeah." Harriet gasped as she read Dierdre's second message. "Especially when, according to Dierdre, Zee is a farm mechanic. And you'll never guess where he works."

"The Kingsbury Estate?"

"Bingo." She texted Dierdre, asking if she'd had a chance to snoop in Zee's van.

"Is this new information to her?" Will pressed. "If she knew earlier, it would explain her reaction to the circle I drew on the map."

Harriet grimaced. "I think it's new information for her, yes. Either way, at least she's telling us now." Harriet read Dierdre's next text then pocketed her phone. "She hasn't had a chance to search Zee's van yet. Maybe we'll get a chance to peek inside it while we're at the estate."

"I don't think that's a good idea," Will said. "Besides, if Zee works on a farm, it'd be easy enough to explain away any evidence of animals in his van. Even transporting laborers about the estate could've tracked stuff inside."

Harriet huffed. "So unless we find the missing sheep or catch these guys in the act of taking more, we have no way to prove who did any of it. Since Zee works on the estate, whoever's behind the scheme wouldn't have to pay him under the table for his extra services. He could say it's for overtime work. They could even pay Tristan directly without raising any eyebrows, since he does part-time work at different farms." Harriet straightened in her chair at a sudden thought. "On the other hand, if we could analyze the estate's payroll records, they might be more telling than whoever's hired Zee realizes."

"We're going to the estate to ramble on the public path, not break into their office and illegally search their accounting records," Will reminded her.

"Yes, of course. But maybe someone we know works on the estate books and could check them for anything fishy. Like if Tristan only shows up on the payroll following thefts, or if Zee earns overtime around the same time. That would be strong circumstantial evidence."

"But for it to stand up in court, the police need a legally defensible suspicion for applying for a search warrant."

Harriet crossed her arms over her chest. "You know what your problem is? You watch too many police procedurals instead of fun little mystery shows."

Will chuckled. "If only we could solve crime as easily as your favorite amateur sleuth."

His laughter cajoled Harriet out of her preoccupation with the case and into a more lighthearted conversation about their favorite books and TV shows.

An hour later, they parked at an entrance to the public pathway that wound across the Kingsbury Estate.

"This is gorgeous," Will said, admiring the view that ranged from mixed forest to rolling pasturelands to heath dotted with evergreen gorse bushes already sporting bright yellow blossoms. "The estate is well known for its grouse hunts. But at least we don't have to worry about wandering into one this time of year."

Scanning the view, Harriet immediately realized how foolishly optimistic she'd been to imagine they might happen upon the stolen sheep while walking the public path. The estate encompassed hundreds of acres. If their Samuel Bishop copycat wanted to hide his prizes, he could easily arrange to do so well away from the public's scrutiny. She slipped her hand into Will's, determined to not let the fact spoil their afternoon.

Will squeezed her hand as they set off on the grassy path side by side. Unlike the grazing lands nearer White Church Bay, there were no gates to pass through, as most of the land wasn't enclosed with rows of drystone walls or bushes. "Do you know how much of the estate is tenanted?" he asked.

"I know of at least three tenant farmers on the estate, but there might be more."

They soon reached a flock of sheep grazing the hillside. Harriet paused to carefully scan them. "None of these are the missing sheep. They're the wrong breeds."

"These are called Moorjocks," Will said. "In the old days, they used to call folks who lived among the moors that too, as cut off from the rest of the world as they were. Like these sheep, they rarely left the patch on which they were born and raised."

"I suppose I had in mind the enclosed pastures like those near the manor house. There's no way our sheep rustlers would release stolen sheep here. They'd wander off."

"You still want to ramble?"

"Of course." Grinning, she impulsively tipped onto her toes and went to plant a kiss on his cheek. Or at least that was her intention, but Will turned his head so suddenly her lips swept over his. She froze, still standing on her tiptoes, as he gazed down at her, a little stunned.

Then his gaze dropped to her lips. Her heart pummelled her ribs as she swayed toward him once more. The next moment, he dipped his head, and their breaths tangled, their lips mere inches apart as their gazes met once more.

Harriet's eyes slid closed as Will's fingers trailed the contour of her chin before gently cradling her head and touching his lips to hers. Too soon, he withdrew a fraction, and smiling, rested his forehead against hers, his thumb lazily trailing across her cheek. "I've been wanting to do that for some time."

"Me too."

Will dipped his head once more.

But before their lips touched, the sound of a gunshot blast ripped them apart.

CHAPTER NINETEEN

Harriet and Will dove to the dirt then scrabbled under the cover of the gorse bushes.

Harriet plucked prickly gorse needles from her palms as another shot blasted nearby—much too near for her liking.

Shifting into a crouch, Will peered around the bush in the direction of the sound.

A faint shout followed by another loud crack soon followed the last.

"It sounds like someone is shooting clay pigeons." Will straightened, offered her a hand, and pulled a gorse twig from her hair when she stood. "In the movies, it's usually fireworks that go off during the couple's first kiss."

Harriet blew a wisp of hair from her face. "At least it wasn't bad guys shooting at us."

"The fact your mind went there tells me it's time to head home and leave the detective work to the police."

Harriet smacked his arm. "I wasn't the only one who thought we were in the line of fire. You dropped to the ground too."

"Sure, but I figured it was a farmer scaring off a fox or stray dog or something."

Harriet patted his arm. "I believe you."

Somehow, she wasn't nearly as eager to hunt for missing sheep in the middle of nowhere, where farmers carried rifles and she'd be lucky to catch a cell phone signal to call for help if one was turned on them.

Since Will needed to review his sermon notes for the morning, he asked for a rain check on Harriet's offer to make dinner.

Harriet felt too fidgety to stay in alone. Aunt Jinny's car was gone, and her house was dark, so no company was to be had there. Harriet opened the fridge and stared at her meager dinner options.

Charlie twined around her leg, and then Maxwell rattled into the kitchen and gazed up at her expectantly.

"I should've picked up groceries when I was at Galloway's this week. Aunt Jinny's probably having supper at Anthony and Olivia's. Enjoying her grandkids." Harriet poured food into the cat's and dog's dishes, grateful she didn't have to give any thought to their meals. Then she whipped up an omelet for herself.

She texted Dierdre after she'd eaten to ask how the kittens were doing and if she needed any help.

No THANKS, Dierdre promptly replied. REGGIE'S HERE. She followed the pronouncement with a string of exuberant emojis that brought a grin to Harriet's face.

Harriet ended their exchange with a thumbs-up emoji. *First love.* She remembered that giddy feeling. She pressed her fingertips to her lips. Who was she kidding? She'd relived it when Will had kissed her. Harriet started her favorite playlist on her phone then lifted

Charlie into her arms and, nuzzling the cat against her cheek, twirled around the kitchen to the music.

Charlie fussed, digging her claws into Harriet's shoulder while attempting to extricate herself from Harriet's hold.

"Okay, okay." Harriet set her on the floor. "Not a dance fan. I get it." She washed up the few dishes and wandered about the house, trying to decide how to spend her free evening. She should work on the magazine article, but between the kiss and the crazy adrenaline from the gunshots, her mind was too frenetic to focus.

The veterinary line rang. Bracing for another night in a cold barn, Harriet manufactured a cheery "hello."

"Dr. Bailey?" greeted a familiar male voice.

"Yes."

"This is Oliver, the librarian you spoke with at White Church Bay Library last week."

"Ah yes, I thought I recognized your voice. How may I help you?"

"Actually, I think I might be able to help you. I've been reading a diary written in the late 1950s by a Mrs. Tupper and came across a reference to Samuel Bishop."

Harriet snatched up a pen and began jotting notes. "You're saying he was still alive?"

"No. Mrs. Tupper writes that she attended a soiree that ended with the telling of ghost stories. She recounts Samuel Bishop's story as you no doubt heard it told, including rumors that a Russian spy killed him for his secrets."

Harriet stopped writing, not sure how Oliver thought the fact the story hadn't changed in almost seventy years helped her. "Did she happen to share anyone's opinion on the theory?"

"Yes. Everyone accepted it as fact, and she felt guilty about not correcting the storyteller. But she didn't think it would be right to betray her late husband's confidence. Apparently, the late Mr. Tupper worked for the Ministry of Food and Agriculture and had enlisted Samuel Bishop in their scheme to develop new breeds following the Second World War."

"She wrote that in the diary?" Harriet blurted, elated at the confirmation that Samuel had accepted the offer he'd written about in his journal even though he clearly hadn't trusted the man who'd made it.

"She did. Her diary is kept in our rare books room, so we can't lend it out, but you're welcome to come in to view it. Or I'd be happy to photocopy the relevant pages for you."

"That would be wonderful."

"She went on to say that although she didn't know what had happened to Samuel, she couldn't help but laugh at the notion that the Soviet Union had sent an assassin to kill him."

"Interesting."

"She writes that Mr. Tupper had been surprised to find new tenants ensconced at Samuel's place the next time he visited. Apparently, he was as baffled as the villagers over why Samuel had disappeared."

Harriet thanked Oliver for sharing his findings then ended the call and stared at the notes she'd made. If her new theory about the sheep rustler's motive proved true, she wasn't sure how she felt about using Samuel's story as a hook. *Desperate Farmer Resurrects a Decades-Old Experiment in Hopes of Saving the Family Farm* would have been a great hook. *Desperate Farmer Resorts to Sheep Rustling to Save the Family Farm* smacked a little too much of tabloid journalism for her taste.

Her thoughts veered to the Danbys and their new venture. She grabbed her camera and her coat and headed for the door. "I'm going to the neighbor's," she announced to Maxwell and Charlie, who'd curled up together in the living room. "Shouldn't be too late."

If she'd been on the ball, she would have popped over in the afternoon while the sun was shining and the crowds were around, to properly capture what they were doing. One day this week, she would have to do that. In the meantime, she could snap a few photos inside the barns and consider which settings to shoot outside. She usually didn't supply photos with her articles, but stock photos wouldn't cut it with this topic.

Doreen greeted Harriet with a warm hug the instant she opened the kitchen door. "We had the most amazing day. Come in." She motioned Harriet to a seat at the kitchen table as she retrieved two cups and the teapot. "Fancy a cuppa?"

"I'd love one. Thanks."

"I'm afraid I can't offer you any scones, because we're completely sold out."

Harriet gaped. "From my freezer too?"

"Yes!" Doreen exclaimed. "A woman from Scarborough loved them so much, she wanted six dozen for an event she's hosting tomorrow."

"That's awesome."

Doreen poured the tea and then emitted a sigh of relief as she sat and rested her feet on the chair beside her. "I'm so glad we're closed tomorrow. I thought I was used to being on my feet all day, but this was brutal. The kids were so tired they've already gone to bed."

"On a Saturday night? Wow. Do you know how many people visited?"

"Hundreds. We couldn't be more pleased. Everyone gushed about it and loved all the photo ops. The weather was perfect, and three lambs were born today—one set of twins and one single. People loved seeing the brand-new lambs."

"That's terrific. The kids will remember days like today for the rest of their lives."

After Doreen exhausted all her stories from their first day, Harriet shared her newest theory on who was stealing sheep and why.

Doreen gasped. "I hadn't heard that Felicity lost Bo Peep. She must be devastated."

Harriet grimaced. "And I can't help feeling responsible. Part of me wants to believe Simon, who'd been helping mend her fences, stole the ewe. But the fact that every incident happened soon after Dierdre and I paid calls is too coincidental for comfort."

"Dierdre's never come here," Doreen pointed out.

"No, but you live next door to the clinic and she's talked to you plenty about your operation here."

Doreen chuckled. "The girl does have an insatiable curiosity. I think it's endearing. Surely you don't think she's had nefarious motives for asking all those questions?"

"No, I don't." Harriet ignored an unexpected twang of doubt. "She seems genuinely curious. But she's also extremely talkative, and I'm afraid someone has been taking advantage of that to tap her for inside information." She sipped her tea. "I'm praying that we can figure out who that someone is before more sheep go missing and that we can recover the others."

Doreen pressed her hand to her heart. "I haven't held out much hope of finding Prince Charming alive after all this time, but if you're right about the thief wanting him for breeding rather than to sell off or worse, then maybe we'll get our happily-ever-after with our little prince after all."

Her optimism eased some of the guilt weighing on Harriet's heart.

Doreen poked Harriet's arm. "Hey, why the long face?"

Harriet sighed. "I may be off the hook for not properly latching farm gates, but my clients won't be any happier to realize it's my fault they were targeted. After all, my intern might be the one spreading that information, whether she means to or not. I wouldn't blame them if they switched vets because of it."

"Nonsense. Everyone is thrilled to have you here, carrying on your grandfather's practice. You've won over so many locals with your skill."

Harriet shook her head. "If Dierdre's brother has been feeding intel to Zee, people might not see her as entirely innocent, no matter how unintentional her actions." *Please, please, please, Lord, let them be unintentional.* "And I'll be equally to blame for bringing her to the farms."

"Folks wouldn't think badly of either of you. Your heart is in the right place. Everyone can see how hard you're working to make sure the rustler is stopped. I heard how you spoke up about the situation at the meeting Thursday night. A couple of farmers called Tom to mention how impressed they were."

Harriet flushed at the kind words. Ironically, they made her feel guiltier. Only this time she felt guilty for assuming the worst about what her neighbors would think of her.

Until this moment, she hadn't realized what a strong tendency she had to make snap judgments. Sure, some of the local farmers had been slow to accept her as a vet when she first arrived. But for the most part, everyone had shown her nothing but kindness in the months since. "I'm sorry. You're right. Please forget I said anything about it."

Doreen reached across the table and squeezed her hand encouragingly. "It's forgotten."

Harriet's phone rang, and she glanced at the screen. "Excuse me, this might be an emergency." She stood and stepped away from the table. "Felicity, what's up?"

"The Shipley lad found our Bo Peep. Isn't that marvelous? I was hoping you could come check her over. To make sure she's okay."

Doreen must have overheard the news, because her face lit up.

"Tristan Shipley?" Harriet clarified.

"Aye."

"Did he say where he found her?"

"He spotted her in a ditch halfway along the carriageway between our places. He was riding with a friend who had a van, and they took her to his place. But thankfully, Dierdre recognized our Bo Peep and sent him here." Felicity's voice trilled with delight. "I hate to bother you on a Saturday night. There isn't anything obviously wrong with her, so if you'd rather wait until tomorrow morning or afternoon, or even Monday." Her tone grew self-recriminating. "It was selfish of me to call and interrupt your evening."

"Not at all," Harriet replied. "Your concern is well founded. I'll be right over."

Felicity sighed with obvious relief. "I'm glad I called then. I want to be sure."

"I'll see you soon."

Doreen smiled as Harriet disconnected the call. "This is an interesting twist."

Harriet had to agree. If Tristan's account of how he'd come to find Bo Peep was true, that made her think he was innocent of wrongdoing. Unfortunately, that would also mean they were back to square one about the identity of the sheep thief. On the other hand, did she really want Dierdre's brother to be guilty?

Either way, while she was glad for the return of one of the missing sheep, she was more at sea about the rest of them than ever before.

CHAPTER TWENTY

I don't know what to think," Harriet admitted to Polly on Monday morning before Dierdre arrived at the clinic. "On one hand, the breeds on the list of stolen sheep were a near identical match to the breeds we deciphered from Samuel's journals, but if their goal is to recreate his alleged super-breed, why return Bo Peep, the only Hampshire Down that was taken?"

"Maybe they knew their alibi for the time of her disappearance wouldn't stand up to scrutiny. Dierdre could've said something to tip them off that you were onto them, and they figured it was better to cut their losses. It potentially cleared their names, and made them look like heroes to boot."

Harriet winced, remembering Dierdre's reaction to the map. Had she wanted to warn Tristan before divulging where Zee worked? "You could be right. Or my suspicions of them could've been totally unfounded in the first place."

"I don't know. They had means and opportunity. And even if their motive is to recreate this super-breed, the motive is ultimately still money."

"The motive sure can't be prestige. Not when the dam's and sire's provenances couldn't be proven."

Polly chuckled. "Your grandfather's gallery is inspiring you to pick up the art world's lingo, I see."

"It's true though. The government's tagging requirements are strict. If someone plans to breed the stolen sheep, he'll have to falsify tags somehow or risk getting caught."

"Maybe he has a friend who's a computer whiz and can adjust things," Polly speculated.

Harriet grinned at the way Polly's eyes lit up when she got swept away with an idea.

"Think about it," Polly insisted. "The thief could keep the same tags on the sheep if the computerized records were changed."

"But the original owners would have their tag numbers recorded outside the system too."

"Sure, but if the thief doesn't sell any of the sheep he's stolen, their numbers won't appear anywhere to throw up flags, right?"

Harriet frowned. "I guess not. Unless the numbers of offspring somehow incorporate their parents' numbers. I'm not sure. We'd be talking a sophisticated fraud."

"Or maybe for the past few years, the mastermind behind all of this has been reporting more lamb births than they've actually had in order to generate tags that they can then use on any sheep they illegally acquire."

Harriet laughed. "Has anyone ever told you that you have a rather creative mind?"

Polly's cheeks turned crimson. "I've been watching a lot of police shows since Van and I broke up."

"Oh yeah? Having second thoughts about that decision?"

Polly lifted one shoulder. "I hate that a good relationship ended, but the idea of being married—let alone to a copper—still scares me."

"I didn't know the fact Van was a police officer was what scared you."

"It wasn't at the time. His proposal came out of the blue, and I didn't know how I felt about any of it. I hadn't even considered the idea of marrying him at that point. In a matter of days, I went from thinking he'd gone off me to a proposal."

"But I don't think you need to be concerned about his job being all that risky."

"No, probably not. It's not like the American cop shows."

Harriet chuckled. "Definitely not, especially in White Church Bay and with his being a detective."

"I do miss spending time with him," Polly admitted.

As if they'd summoned him, Van strode through the door.

"There's been another development that might disprove your theory," he announced after they'd exchanged good mornings. "A lamb was stolen from a farm near Scarborough last night."

"That doesn't make sense. Why would they want one so young?"

"If it hasn't been tagged yet, the thief can claim it as offspring of one of his own sheep," Polly said. "It's a neat way to avoid the tagging issue we talked about. What breed was it, Van?"

"A Romney."

Harriet frowned. "Not a breed on Samuel's list."

"And not within the radius of Kingsbury Estate that you and the pastor narrowed down," Van added, clearly frustrated by the ill-fitting development.

After securing a Lonk farmer's tentative agreement the previous afternoon, Harriet and Will had laid out their evidence and theory to Van. With a bit of finagling, they had secured the go-ahead from Van's superiors for a sting.

"Maybe the lamb theft wasn't the work of our rustlers," Polly suggested. "Maybe it's another person or group."

"We considered that," Van said, crossing his arms over his chest. "But the discrepancy has my boss second-guessing investing manpower into your sting plan."

Polly's eyes widened. "What sting plan?"

Harriet filled her in.

"Then maybe making you question the theory was exactly what the rustlers wanted," Polly said.

Harriet sucked in a breath. "Dierdre was the only other person who knew about our theory of the radius of the crimes."

"If Dierdre tipped them off," Polly speculated, "they could've deliberately targeted a farm outside of the radius, hoping you'd question your theory and start chasing your tails."

Van's eyes crinkled with amusement. "You're right. I felt like a dog chasing his tail when I got the news this morning."

"But are we still okay to visit the Lonk farm today, as we discussed? The Johnsons agreed to the wellness check on their flock."

"Aye. The DI has allocated two undercover officers to tail Shipley and his pal for up to three days after we hear from you."

"Great." Harriet held up crossed fingers. "Here's hoping we haven't spooked them into lying low for a while."

"Aye," Polly agreed. "Or nicking their Lonks from a field in another area, where they're less likely to be missed."

"Don't say that," Harriet begged. The last thing she wanted was for Van to change his mind about their sting idea. His boss, Detective

Inspector Kerry McCormick, had waffled a long while before agreeing. If she caught so much as a whiff that Van's confidence had wavered, she might still pull the plug.

Dierdre entered with the box of kittens. "What's going on?"

"Nothing," Polly said too loudly, turning to her computer.

"There's been another sheep theft," Harriet said, hoping Dierdre wouldn't wonder about Polly's strange reaction. "And unfortunately, it pretty much blitzes my theory."

Dierdre's eyes widened. "You don't think"—she shot a sideways glance at Van—"it's who you thought it was?" she finished cryptically.

"Don't worry, Miss Shipley," Van reassured her. "Dr. Bailey has apprised us of the possibility that Zee Goodfellow tapped your brother for information on local farms that you might've shared with him."

Zee's last name was Goodfellow? If he was indeed behind the sheep thefts, Harriet found that rather ironic.

Dierdre tightened her grip on the box of kittens. "Tristan couldn't have known what Zee was doing with the information. He wouldn't condone stealing. You have to believe me. He even returned one he found on the road. Did you hear about that?"

"Yes, I did." Harriet patted her arm reassuringly. "And the police know how hard he works for the farmers in the area."

"It's natural that he and Zee would talk about local farms, since they both work on them. Tris wouldn't think anything was wrong with Zee asking him questions about my farm visits, would he?"

"Not at all," Harriet agreed soothingly. "Did you happen to mention to Tristan our theory about the thefts all being within a certain radius of Kingsbury Estate?"

"I didn't tell anyone about that." Dierdre pressed her lips together as a frantic-looking woman burst through the door, leading a woebegone Irish setter.

Van excused himself as Polly asked the potential client what brought her in.

Lowering her voice, Dierdre said to Harriet, "Since I learned Zee worked at the Kingsbury Estate, I haven't said another word to either of them about anything."

"You might not want to stop talking altogether about your work here. They might find that suspicious too."

She shook her head. "I never thought of that. I'll only talk about office appointments then."

"Good thinking," Harriet agreed. "Go ahead and get the kittens settled in the office, then wash your hands and join me in the exam room."

Dierdre nodded and hurried away, her expression tight.

Harriet smiled at Siobhan O'Connor, who explained that her Irish setter had been listless and not eating for the last day or so. "You can bring Suzie straight through." Harriet motioned to the door on the left then grabbed the file folder Polly held out to her.

Joining the pair in the exam room, Harriet knelt beside Suzie to check her over. "How long ago did she have pups?"

"Five weeks."

Harriet took her temperature. "She does have a bit of a fever, which could indicate an infection, along with the other symptoms you've mentioned. We'll give her antibiotics and an injection to bring down her temperature."

Dierdre slipped into the room, and Harriet made introductions.

"Suzie should start feeling better in no time," Harriet explained while she prepared the injections. "But you'll need to keep her from the puppies until the medication is out of her system. You can feed them warmed, canned puppy food and formula. Keep them under heat lamps or on a heating pad to help them stay warm, and check on them more than you normally would if their mother was with them."

"How many puppies did she have?" Dierdre asked.

Siobhan grimaced. "Eight."

"Don't worry. They'll be okay." Dierdre stroked Suzie's fur. "I'm hand-raising four newborn kittens at the moment. Having siblings for them to snuggle with helps a lot to keep them warm."

"It does indeed," Harriet confirmed.

"But Suzie will be okay?" Siobhan asked.

"She should be, yes. If you have any concerns, bring her straight back," Harriet instructed. "And feel free to call if you have any questions. We're not leaving you to deal with this all by yourself."

"Thank you," Siobhan said fervently.

After walking Siobhan and Suzie to reception, Harriet commended Dierdre on her excellent bedside manner.

"I rescheduled this morning's last two office visits," Polly told them when Siobhan left. "You're needed at a farm on the other side of Whitby. A cow caught in a bog."

Harriet raised an eyebrow. "That sounds like a job for a tow truck."

"A tractor and a winch, actually," Dierdre interjected. "It happened to one of my uncle's cows last summer. At least you won't have to worry about the cow kicking you when you're messing about with securing the straps around her, because her legs are likely good and stuck in the mud."

"And in this temperature, if we don't get her out quick, she's going to succumb to hypothermia. We better get moving." Harriet grabbed a complete change of clothes so they could carry on to the Lonk farm as soon as the cow was stable.

For once, Harriet's GPS didn't give her any trouble, and they located the farm in record time. Still, by the time she drove across the bone-rattling terrain as close to the scene as she could get, the bellowing cow had sunk up to its neck in black muck.

A lone woman was next to the beast, straining to secure a rope around it.

"Make a bowline loop," Dierdre called to her. "It's the easiest to untie afterward."

Harriet hoped the woman knew what a bowline was, or she might have to do a search on her cell phone. Harriet glanced toward the unoccupied tractor parked on higher ground. "Are you the only one here?"

"Aye," the woman said. "No sooner did my husband get called to help with a lifeboat rescue than I spotted this one in the bog, the daft thing. I rang him, but he'd already pushed off with the rescue team."

"It's okay. We can do this," Dierdre said optimistically. "Slip the loop over the cow's head and behind her ears. Then we can watch her from here, while you operate the tractor. We'll signal you when to move and to slow or speed up."

"Won't the rope choke her if I loop it around her head?" the woman asked.

"If you position the knot under her jaw, so we're pulling on her neck rather than her throat, she'll be okay," Harriet assured her. "The pressure should distribute evenly across the back of the skull and neck. Ideally, we'd position a second rope around her rear end to give her an added shove. But I've heard of cows being dragged out of ponds with logging chains looped around their necks, and they were none the worse for wear by the next day."

Dierdre clapped her hands. "Let's do this. That cow's getting colder by the second."

The woman ran up the hill, and thirty seconds later, the tractor roared to life.

Harriet signaled her to start moving. At first, the tractor struggled to gain traction. "Maybe we should use the winch instead," Harriet said to Dierdre, who clearly had more experience with such scenarios.

"Give it another minute," Dierdre said. They both continued to encourage the cow to remain calm.

A moment later, a great sucking sound erupted, and the cow's shoulders emerged. Then the tractor tires began throwing mud, and the progress halted.

"Are you sure this will work?" Harriet asked her intern.

"It'll work," Dierdre insisted. She raced halfway up the hill to a position that allowed her a view of both the cow and the tractor. She made hand signals Harriet couldn't interpret, but apparently the woman could.

"Hold up a second," Harriet shouted. "Give her a chance to catch her breath." Once the cow seemed a little calmer, Harriet signaled again. "Okay, keep going."

Once the cow was halfway out, she started trying to pull herself out and was soon free of her prison. Dierdre ran back down the hill and removed the chain from her neck.

"Easy, girl. Easy," Harriet soothed, patting her back, but the cow startled and took off like a bullet. Shaking her head, Harriet trudged up the hill to speak to the farmer.

"She'll be off to the cowhouse," the woman predicted. "I'll meet you over there, shall I? I'd like you to examine her before you leave."

"Of course." Harriet and Dierdre climbed into the Beast, having managed to stay relatively clean, considering. They soon verified that the rescued cow was fine, advised the woman to hose her down with warm water then dry her. Then they headed off to the Johnsons' farm.

"What exactly does a wellness check involve?" Dierdre asked as they settled into the drive.

Harriet spent the remainder of the time detailing what they'd be looking for in the animals and in the farm's care routines to see if they could offer any recommendations.

It was the perfect kind of visit to feed Dierdre's curiosity. Hopefully she'd leave bubbling over with so much new information that she couldn't help but share it with her family.

But as if Dierdre had read Harriet's mind, she said, "Don't worry, I won't say anything to Tristan about the sheep farm. I can tell him about the cow rescue though, right?"

"Of course."

Dierdre fussed with her fingernails, avoiding Harriet's gaze. "Do you really still think Tristan could've tipped off Zee from my stories? Even after they returned Bo Peep?"

"To be honest, I don't know what to think. We only have their word that they found Bo Peep and didn't just pretend to."

Dierdre's gaze snapped to Harriet. "Tristan wouldn't lie about something like that. In fact, he's a terrible liar. We can always tell when he's trying to put one over on us."

"Was he with Zee when they spotted Bo Peep?"

"Yeah, Zee had picked him up to take him to the pub for a darts match."

"So Zee could've released Bo Peep in the ditch before arriving to collect Tristan," Harriet theorized.

Dierdre gasped. "I never thought of that. Are the police watching him?"

Harriet hesitated, unsure how wise it would be to confirm anything. What if Zee decided to put his plan on hold for a while? Although if Dierdre wondered if the police were watching him, Zee likely was too.

"Sorry, I guess you wouldn't know, would you?" Dierdre went on. "I was thinking about who else I talk to sometimes about our farm visits, and that's Ian. He's my lab partner in biology."

Harriet racked her brain. Why did that name sound familiar?

"He said Simon Boyes is staying at his house."

Harriet had to swallow a groan of frustration. Instead of clearing suspects, she apparently seemed to be finding more reasons to be suspicious of them. "Did you happen to ask Ian if he shares your farm stories with Simon?"

"No. It didn't cross my mind that I'd shared them with him until after Tristan and Zee found Bo Peep, which made me think Zee couldn't be the thief."

"Maybe you're right. Except it doesn't sound as if Simon has access to transportation."

"Ian drives him some places." Dierdre frowned. "But he wouldn't let Simon nick a sheep and transport it in the family van."

Harriet chuckled at a mental image of a sheep poking its nose between the front seats and bleating at Ian's mom. "You're right. I can't imagine him getting away with that."

Still, as much as it would pain Will, this was another possible clue that might point toward Simon.

CHAPTER TWENTY-ONE

The next couple of days passed with no new thefts and no new clues on either front. Harriet managed to reach Walter Devon from the Ministry of Agriculture. But he didn't offer any hope that having the name Mr. Tupper as Samuel Bishop's contact would enable them to find information about him any faster.

After Wednesday night's small group study, as Harriet stood in the church parking lot chatting with Will and fellow congregants, Van drove in and asked to speak to her and Will alone.

Of course, Will's invitation for Van to join them for coffee at the parsonage set the others to whispering.

Will's warm hand at the small of Harriet's back soothed her agitation over suddenly becoming the topic of their conversation. As they settled at Will's kitchen table, Van pushed his coffee aside, untouched. "I'm afraid I have bad news. The auctioneer's office clerk couldn't identify who rummaged through their records a few months ago."

"Did you show her pictures?" Will asked.

"Aye. She was positive it wasn't Zee, but uncertain whether it might've been either Simon or Tristan."

"But they look nothing alike," Harriet protested.

"Which is why DI McCormick has concluded she isn't a reliable witness. And after tonight, she's pulling the plug on allocating officers to follow our suspects, who at the moment appear to be tucked into their homes for the night."

Harriet groaned. "Dierdre must've let something slip that spooked them. I think that's why they returned Bo Peep—to try to throw us off their scent."

Will reached across the table and squeezed her hand. "The night's still young. They might be waiting to sneak out in the wee hours." He turned his attention to Van. "Will you leave the security cameras up at the Johnson farm regardless?"

"For another week or so, just in case. We tried to mount them in the most likely places a rustler would park to access the fields, but the perimeter is too vast to properly monitor it without a lot more cameras than we can afford."

Harriet clenched her hand into a fist. "This has to work. How can we know what's going on and not catch these guys? We must be missing something."

Will topped off his mug. "My housekeeper knows the house-keeper at Kingsbury Estate. I've asked her to find out who the book-keeper is. If we talk to him or her, maybe we can confirm your theory about extra payments being made to Zee, and possibly Tristan or Simon, that coincide with the dates of the thefts."

Van plugged his ears. "I'm not hearing this."

"If you got a warrant to search their financial records, we could make short work of getting that answer," Harriet told him.

"Except the law requires *evidence* to justify a warrant," he reminded her.

"Evidence that we apparently can't get without a warrant. It's a vicious circle," Will lamented.

"Don't worry. We're not giving up on the case." Van rubbed the back of his neck. After a moment he said, "We found out who took the lamb in Scarborough. Some woman's ex-boyfriend pinched it to impress his new girlfriend. Between that and the Barneses' Hampshire Down appearing to have simply wandered off, the DI's belief that the rest of the disappearances are connected is fading fast."

"You had another theory about Bo Peep," Will reminded Harriet. "Tell him."

Harriet straightened in her chair. "A farmer trying to recreate Samuel Bishop's breeding program would've been after male Hampshire Downs, not females. Samuel made notes of which gender he used from each breed for the best results."

Will leaned back in his chair. "And if whoever hired Zee and Tristan refused to pay for their mistake, they could've figured returning Bo Peep was a good way to take the scrutiny off themselves if they'd caught wind they were suspects."

"Maybe." Van stared at his untouched coffee. "But why would someone want to resurrect Bishop's breed when there are plenty of fine newer breeds available these days? It was never even proven to exist, was it?"

"Not that I found any evidence of," Harriet conceded. Had she taken her fascination with Samuel's story too far? Merely spun it into a fantastic tale that had nothing whatsoever to do with the sheep rustling?

And if her theory was wrong, then what was actually going on?

The next couple of days were uneventfully routine. Dierdre accompanied Harriet on farm calls. The kittens continued to thrive under her care.

Friday evening, Harriet chatted with Will on the phone before working on the magazine article some more. The pictures she'd taken at the Danbys' and other farms provided ample inspiration for the bulk of the article, but she continued to waver over how to write the opening hook.

She wished she knew what had become of Samuel Bishop. Thoughts of his story set her thinking about the thefts again. Were they connected to his breeding strategy? Or was her preoccupation with his story making her see connections where there weren't any? Was she as guilty of wild speculation as the folks who'd started the assassination rumors about him?

After all, beyond circumstantial evidence, she had no proof that Tristan and Zee had anything to do with the thefts. According to Van, they'd spent their evenings at the pub since they'd been under surveillance. And Simon had taken a job at a local gas station, working five to midnight every night.

Harriet couldn't shake the feeling that somewhere along the line, she'd missed a vital clue. This wasn't over—not by a long shot.

Saturday morning dawned as dreary as Harriet's mood, but she did her best to put on a pleasant smile. It was the last day of half-term break and the last day she'd be working with Dierdre.

Dierdre beamed at Harriet as she bounced into the clinic. "Are you going to miss me after today?"

"I am. You've been a wonderful asset, and you're welcome to join me again anytime."

Dierdre fiddled with a strand of hair, curling it around her finger as color rose to her cheeks. "You mean it? All my talking didn't drive you crazy?"

"Not at all. And I'd be happy to write you a glowing recommendation for veterinary college. You'll make a wonderful vet someday."

Dierdre stood a few inches taller, her expression even brighter than when she'd walked in. "You don't know how much that means to me, Dr. Bailey."

"It's my pleasure."

Polly waved a piece of paper to snag their attention. "And my gift to you is that I saved two farm calls for your last day. Mr. Wellington has a cow that's about to give birth, and he'd like you there to supervise. There's also a Shire horse that needs its teeth floated." Floating a horse's teeth referred to a procedure where the sharp points of the teeth were removed. It gave the horse's teeth an even grinding pattern while chewing, which helped with their digestion.

"A Shire?" Harriet's voice rose with surprise. "Who has heavy horses like those around here?" A handful of independent breweries continued the tradition of using draught horses to pull delivery wagons, but none in this vicinity.

Polly's eyes gleamed. "The Kingsbury Estate. They use the Shire for pleasure riding mostly, but he also pulls wagons in a couple of local parades and is a great addition to their petting zoo."

"Seriously?" Harriet's heart hammered. Maybe the day was looking up after all. Seeing to a horse on the estate was a prime opportunity to do more nosing about. She slanted a glance at Dierdre and couldn't decide whether or not to take it as a good sign that the prospect of returning there didn't appear to make her nervous.

Harriet added a step stool to the Beast since Shires tended to be gigantic. Thankfully, their easygoing temperament more than compensated for their intimidating size.

They drove to the Wellington farm first, where the Jersey cow gave birth without a hitch. While Harriet saw to the new mother, Dierdre, in her usual fashion, pummeled the farmer with a slew of questions about everything from his breeding scheme to vaccination schedules. In fact, by the time they packed up their equipment to leave, Mr. Wellington appeared more impressed with the eager student than his strapping new calf.

"I'm sorry," Dierdre said as they set off to Kingsbury Estate. "I was talking too much again, wasn't I?"

"Not at all. Mr. Wellington clearly enjoyed sharing his farming philosophy with you." Harriet nudged up the truck's heat. "It's funny. I've always thought Yorkshire farmers were rather taciturn, but you have a knack for getting them talking."

They drove in silence for a few miles with Dierdre gazing out her window. Then she twisted in her seat to face Harriet. "Do the police still think Zee's connected to the sheep rustling?"

Harriet glanced over at her. "Do you?"

"No. I don't think so. My brother's a good guy. He never ran with the wrong crowd, never got in trouble at school. I trust his judgment. And he enjoys Zee's company. Zee even got him some work at the Kingsbury Estate."

Harriet sucked in a breath at the confirmation Tristan had been paid—or perhaps paid off—by someone at the estate. Taking a few slow breaths in through her nose, Harriet waited for her suddenly rampaging pulse to slow before asking, "What does he do there?"

"Oh, it's *so* cute," Dierdre gushed. "He and Bouncer are doing herding demonstrations with the sheep. It started out as a one-off for the lord of the manor's son's birthday party last month. Then one of the party guests suggested bringing Tristan in during half-term to teach the kids how to train their dogs."

"Sounds like fun."

"Tris loves it. Herding sheep with dogs is one of the annual events at the Yorkshire Fair every year, so I'm sure he's inspired a few boys to have a go at it. Maybe it'll lead to some private training gigs for him. I hope so. He's a born teacher."

To hear Dierdre talk about her brother, Harriet hated to imagine him culpable in the sheep-rustling incidents. She'd been an only child, but among all her friends growing up, she'd never known any who thought so highly of their big brother as Dierdre.

Once at the stables, Harriet administered mild sedation to the Shire and inserted a mouth guard to ensure it didn't bite her as she worked. Smoothing the sharp points off the sweet gray's teeth then proved to be quick work. "His back tooth doesn't have a match." She invited Dierdre to compare the molars from top to bottom. "Without one, a tooth becomes excessively overgrown." To the groomsman, she advised more frequent checks to avoid complications.

After they'd packed their equipment in the Beast, Dierdre spotted the farm manager and dashed over to him to secure permission to watch Tristan at work.

Harriet took the opportunity to text Will about the newest development. The manager directed them to a patch behind the manor where Tristan held the children and their dogs in rapt attention.

The lord of the manor, a handsome fortysomething man with dark hair and an easy smile, joined them. "It's a treat to watch, isn't it?" He held his hand out to Harriet then Dierdre. "I'm Neal Bourgo, by the way."

"It is," Harriet agreed. She introduced herself and Dierdre. Watching Tristan with the children, she understood why Dierdre couldn't believe her brother had anything to do with the sheep rustling. And given the number of children under his charge, he honestly earned whatever paycheck the Kingsbury Estate cut him.

"We've raised sheep on the estate for as long as I can remember," Neal mused. "I remember spending time with the shepherds as a young boy and being fascinated by how they and their dogs guided the sheep with little more than a blast of their whistle or a short command. I secretly wished I could be a shepherd."

"I suspect most boys long for a special bond like those between shepherds and their dogs."

"Very true," he agreed. "I'm glad I asked my son if it was something he'd like to do. Working with the dog has really boosted his confidence."

"That's lovely to hear." Harriet wondered if hosting workshops for children and their dogs might be one of those unconventional revenue streams Tristan could explore to help make working the family farm a viable option for him.

Not wanting to let the opportunity to do a little more sleuthing pass, Harriet asked, "Do you only have Blackface sheep on the estate these days?"

"On the main estate, yes. But one of our tenant farmers has diversified."

"Oh? What breeds does he raise?"

"Leicester Longwool and Texel."

It suddenly occurred to Harriet that perhaps the reason the Johnsons' Lonks weren't stolen was because whoever acquired the stolen sheep already had sufficient Lonk stock of his own. Doing her best to sound only mildly curious, she asked, "All good breeds. Do they keep any Lonk?"

He cocked his head, as if remembering something. "Are you the young vet who came by a couple of weeks ago inquiring about Samuel Bishop's flock?"

Her heart thudded in her chest. The mere mention of Lonk sheep had sent his mind there? "You heard about that?" She cleared her throat so her voice would stop squeaking. "Yes, that was me."

"Did you find what you were looking for?"

She hesitated. What if his reason for asking wasn't born of idle curiosity? "We found his journals, but making sense of them was another matter." She explained how she'd hoped to use his story as a hook for her article. "One of his journals mentions that he was asked to participate in a breeding scheme. Did the estate abandon the pursuit after he vanished?"

"I've never heard anything about that. The world was a mess in those days. Government positions were continually shuffled, with folks emigrating in droves. If the government pulled funding, the estate might have reverted back to tried-and-true methods to rebuild the stock lost to that terrible blizzard."

"Understandable. It's been lovely to meet you." Harriet nudged Dierdre's elbow. "We should get going."

"Why were you in such a hurry to get away?" Dierdre asked as they climbed into the truck.

"Did you notice how he didn't actually answer my question about raising Lonks?"

Dierdre crinkled her nose. "So?"

Harriet hadn't let Dierdre in on the significance of the breeds stolen for fear she might let that information slip to Tristan. But the way his lordship had ignored Harriet's question in favor of asking whether she had been inquiring about Samuel Bishop set off all kinds of alarm bells.

CHAPTER TWENTY-TWO

Harriet's palms were sweating by the time they left the estate. "You said your boyfriend lives around here?" she asked Dierdre, thinking he might know if any of Kingsbury's tenant farmers raised Lonks.

"He does. Why do you ask?"

"I'd like to pay him a visit."

Dierdre frowned. "I'm not sure he'd be very happy if we just show up. Like I said, he's paranoid about biosecurity."

"I want to ask him what he knows about the breeds raised by Kingsbury's tenant farmers."

"Do you think one of them is behind the thefts?" Dierdre asked. "And that Neal Bourgo knows?"

"I don't know what to think." Harriet focused on the road. "I'd like to gather more facts before I decide anything."

"Reggie would probably be okay with talking to you. But please don't get him in trouble with the lord of the manor. He's working so hard to make something of his grandfather's farm. Bad blood between neighbors, especially powerful neighbors like a lord, wouldn't be good." Dierdre motioned to the road. "Take a right here, and I'll call Reggie." At the following corner, she directed Harriet to go left. "He's not answering." Dierdre tapped out a text message.

Noticing a flock of Lonk sheep, Harriet's excitement grew. "Do you know who owns that flock?"

"Aye, Reggie's grandfather. They're the hefted lot I told you about, but he planted hedgerows around the fields to hem them in. It feels more secure."

"How close a watch do Reggie and his grandfather keep on their flocks?"

Dierdre's hand stilled over her cell phone, and her gaze snapped to Harriet's. "Do you think they might have been targeted?" Anxiety laced her voice. "I told Reggie about the other missing sheep from the first. I'm sure he's keeping close tabs on all their animals."

Slowing her truck, Harriet drew alongside the field. "I have reason to believe that our thief might be interested in acquiring Lonks. That's why Neal Bourgo's reaction to my question bothered me."

Dierdre shuddered. "Maybe we should take a head count."

Harriet parked on the side of the road, and they both climbed out to count sheep. It wasn't the easiest task, since the animals could be difficult even for pros to distinguish. On their first attempt, they came up with two different numbers and had to try again. The second time, their counts matched.

Dierdre began tapping another message on her cell phone. "I'll ask Reggie how many should be here. Some might have wandered into the valley and be hidden by the gorse bushes. Do you think we should walk down there?"

"Let's see what Reggie has to say first." While they waited for his response, Harriet drove the rest of the way to the farm, a sprawling collection of old stone barns.

"He still hasn't answered." Dierdre squinted toward the main barn.

Another suspicion pricked Harriet's mind. "Has Reggie enjoyed hearing about your veterinary exploits over the past few weeks?" she asked, striving to sound as if she were merely making conversation.

Dierdre smiled dreamily as she exited the Land Rover. "Aye. Mum says we're like two peas in a pod. He's the only bloke she's met that's as inquisitive as I am."

Harriet forced a chuckle to mask her growing suspicion. Like Tristan, Reggie had been privy to all of Dierdre's inside information on local farms. But unlike Tristan and his friend Zee, Reggie had a farm and was highly motivated to improve on what his grandfather had established. Moreover, he lived within minutes of Kingsbury Estate, the apparent center point of the thefts. And he already had Lonk, which meant he had no reason to target the Johnson farm.

Dierdre pointed to the open door of the closest barn. "He's probably in there. I'm sure he won't mind our walking that far and calling to him."

"Sounds good." Harriet scanned the other barns, wondering where he might hide stolen sheep if her suspicion proved true. Signs warning visitors not to enter for biosecurity were posted on every door. Dierdre hadn't been exaggerating Reggie's standards.

Or was the appearance of fastidiousness his way of keeping people from finding out that he might be covering up something more nefarious?

Dierdre hurried ahead of Harriet, calling Reggie's name.

From inside the barn, a male voice snapped, "What are you doing here?"

The two women entered the barn, and Dierdre shot Harriet an apologetic look then explained to Reggie why they'd come.

"Wait outside," he grumbled. "I'll be with you as soon as I get this filthy bedding cleared away. We had two more lambs born this afternoon, and we can't afford a lapse in hygienic measures."

Harriet admired the otherwise-immaculate state of the barn's interior and couldn't blame the young man for his concern. "I'll wander around out here while we wait," she said to Dierdre, before moving away from the door.

Dierdre joined her outside the barn. "Sorry about that. He gets super-focused when he's in the middle of something, and doesn't like being distracted."

"I understand." Harriet shrugged as if it was no big deal, though she didn't appreciate Reggie's tone toward someone he professed to care about. Was he always so short-tempered with Dierdre, or had they startled him in the middle of a task he didn't want anyone to know about? Either way, Harriet wasn't impressed with her intern's beau thus far. "I was surprised to see only one other lamb in there besides the two newborns. I thought he rushed home Thursday night because a ewe was in labor. And then he didn't spend Valentine's Day with you because another was due."

Dierdre frowned. "That's right. Well, he did bring me flowers on Valentine's Day, but he didn't stay long. I was kind of freaking out about my grandparents' flock being targeted next, so I probably heard wrong when he said why he needed to get going."

As in maybe he needed to stake out the Barneses' farm to score a prizewinning Hampshire Down? Then on Valentine's Day, he'd discovered his steal was the wrong gender.

Perhaps Reggie was the one who'd released Bo Peep. He could have done it in the hope that having one of the missing sheep appear to be an escapee would cast doubt on the whole sheep-rustling theory the farming community was up in arms about.

"You're not still worried about your grandparents' flock?" Harriet asked Dierdre.

"Dad put up wildlife cameras and said that was the best they could do for the time being." Dierdre hitched her thumb toward the barn door. "I'll hang around here until Reggie's ready."

"No problem." Harriet needed a few moments to reassess her suspicions and slow her racing pulse. Strolling from fold to fold, she scanned the ewes grouped according to due dates, although she kept her distance so as not to raise Reggie's ire. When she returned to the ancient stone barns, she peeked around the half-open door of the one on the end and caught sight of a pair of sheep unlike the ones she'd seen in Reggie's folds.

Her pulse quickened all over again.

Sheep preferred to stay outdoors because of their thick wool coats, even in inclement weather. If these were new acquisitions, quarantining them for a couple of weeks was a wise procedure. However, given Reggie's extreme biosecurity measures, she doubted he'd risk acquiring outside animals in the middle of lambing season, even if he quarantined them in a separate building.

Unless they weren't acquired legally, and his biosecurity narrative was nothing but smoke and mirrors.

She glanced at Dierdre, still patiently waiting for Reggie. He could simply be concerned about the sheeps' health. Expert farmers rarely called in a vet to examine an ill animal, because they were used to dealing with all kinds of issues themselves.

Of course, since she was here and he was Dierdre's friend, she could offer to look them over at no cost. She moved closer to the pair of sheep, and her breath caught.

Even with her limited experience with uniquely British breeds, there was no mistaking this one. It was the same breed that had been stolen from the Fairburns, and the two looked like ewes, which was what the Fairburns had lost. It didn't mean he had taken them, but it was awfully coincidental.

Did Dierdre know what her boyfriend might be up to?

Harriet gasped at another thought. Was that why Dierdre had been so quick to point fingers at Mr. Wilcox? To divert their attention from her boyfriend?

Harriet stole closer to the barn door and snapped a picture of the pair of sheep then sent it to Will, along with a text—THESE ARE AT DIERDRE'S BOYFRIEND'S, ONLY ONES OF THIS BREED I CAN FIND HERE. COULD BE THE FAIRBURNS' MISSING GIMMERS. WILL TRY TO FIND SHEEP THAT MATCH THE DESCRIPTIONS OF THE OTHERS.

Dierdre called her name. Harriet stuffed her phone into her pocket and sauntered around from behind the barn, striving for a nonchalant expression so as not to give away what she'd discovered. Because even if Dierdre was oblivious to what Reggie might be up to, her affection for him might cloud the issue for her.

Reggie strode from the barn, his eyes narrowing angrily. "Didn't you see the biosecurity signs? No one is supposed to go past them without permission."

"Sorry about that. I was admiring your sheep. They look wonderfully healthy."

He thanked her for the compliment, but his posture remained stiff, and the muscle in his jaw twitched as he steered them back toward the Land Rover. "Dierdre says you were asking about whether tenant farmers with the Kingsbury Estate raise Lonk and whether any of my grandfather's sheep have gone missing. Is that correct?"

"That's right."

"I can't speak for the tenant farmers. I know which one has the largest holding around here, but he has no Lonks that I'm aware of. My grandfather had fifty head of Lonk, but he lost two over the winter."

"Stolen?" Harriet asked.

"No. Died of old age."

Reggie's cool demeanor worried Harriet. Did he somehow know that she suspected him? Was he trying to throw her off?

"Why don't you show Harriet your five-year plan and charts for all your protocols?" Dierdre suggested. "She might be able to offer some valuable insights."

"I'd be happy to." Harriet shrugged, hoping to give the impression that his agreement didn't matter to her one way or the other. That she wasn't itching to peek into every barn on the property. "No charge, since you're a friend of Dierdre's."

To her surprise, Reggie led the way to the main barn.

This building proved safe for him to show off. It contained ewes that were due to give birth soon along one side and new mamas with their lambs in separate pens along the other. He led her to his office and showed her piles of charts and records he kept on every sheep he and his grandfather owned.

Harriet took her time studying them, hoping he'd slipped up and she'd find a record of a few illegally acquired sheep. But no such luck.

Dierdre excused herself to run to the house for a glass of water. A few moments later, they left his office and Harriet saw that one of the ewes looked like it was going into labor. "I'll need to ask you to leave," Reggie said. "It seems we have another lamb about to arrive."

Harriet plastered on a warm smile. "It sure does. Would you like any help with it?"

"Thanks for the offer, but I don't anticipate any trouble with this birth."

"In that case, I'll go find Dierdre and we'll get out of your hair."

Reggie tensed at the suggestion, appearing to waver over allowing her to leave the barn unescorted. But his farmer's work ethic won out, and he gave the ewe his full attention.

Harriet slipped outside. She squinted toward the house but didn't see any sign of Dierdre. She might never get another chance like this again. She skirted the main barn to slip into the neighboring one.

Except that its door was padlocked. Were Reggie and his grandfather worried about whatever was in that barn going missing with the rash of sheep rustlers in the area?

Or was Reggie hiding that he was behind it all?

She circled the small building in search of another entrance. There was none, nor were there any windows. Perhaps it was merely a storage shed.

She hurried on to the next barn and found it unlocked. Slipping inside, she paused a moment to give her eyes a chance to adjust to the dim light. Unlike the main barn, this one contained a row of horse stalls, with no horses in sight. She hurried down the center aisle, peeking into each stall in turn. At the face in the third stall, she jumped.

"Well, hello there, handsome." Using her cell phone, Harriet snapped a pic of the Suffolk who'd lifted his head at the sound of her voice. "Everyone's been searching for you, Your Highness."

Prince Charming confirmed her observation with a wink. He flicked an ear into a sunbeam, showing off his telltale freckle.

"I'm glad to see you're no worse for wear." She sent the picture to Will and Van with the caption. I'VE FOUND OUR SHEEP RUSTLER. REGGIE SPRINGFIELD. She groaned at the realization she hadn't paid attention to the name of the road, nor whether the farm had its actual address displayed. HIS FARM IS NEAR THE KINGSBURY ESTATE.

Hearing a noise behind her, Harriet tapped Send, shoved the phone back into her pocket, and spun around.

Reggie stood between her and the door, wielding a pitchfork. "What are you doing in here?"

CHAPTER TWENTY-THREE

Surreptitiously scanning for another escape route, Harriet squared her shoulders and held her ground. The man obviously knew she was onto him. She raised her chin. "The more pertinent question is, what is this ram doing here? And how do you think you're going to get away with it?"

Narrowing his eyes, he advanced toward her, pitchfork extended. "I don't know what you think you know, lady, but you're trespassing."

Raising her hands, Harriet backed away from him. "Step aside, and I'll be happy to leave."

His snort communicated loud and clear that he had no intention of doing any such thing. "Too late for that. You're not going anywhere."

"Are you kidding me?" Harriet demanded with more bravado than she felt. "Someone will wonder where I am."

His eyes darkened.

"In that scenario, being exposed as a sheep rustler will be the least of your problems," she continued. "I suppose it was you who searched through the records at the livestock auction?" She prayed he was as chatty as Dierdre and that she could keep him talking until help arrived. "Did you consult Samuel Bishop's journals at the estate too?" She hesitated to warn Reggie that she'd already called the police, since the news might make him desperate—and dangerous.

Please Lord, let Will and Van have seen my text and already be on their way.

"Reggie? Harriet?" Dierdre's voice drifted through the barn's half-open door.

"In here," Harriet shouted. "Reggie's the thief! Call—"

"Shut up," he snarled. "You don't want me to hurt her, do you?"

Harriet clamped her mouth shut.

"She doesn't have a clue what I'm doing," he bit out between clenched teeth, as if he could read the question in Harriet's mind. "She'd never understand what it takes to keep a family farm going these days."

"Glad to hear she's innocent. Aiding and abetting a thief would seriously derail her career plans. If you surrender now and return all the stolen animals, I imagine the worst you'll get is a fine and maybe a short jail sentence, but then you'll be able to continue farming. And that's what you really want anyway."

"There you are." Dierdre strode into the barn. Her smile quickly morphed into wide-eyed confusion. "Reggie, why are you pointing that pitchfork at Harriet?"

Hearing the sound of an approaching car engine, Harriet threw caution to the wind. "Your boyfriend was about to explain what Prince Charming is doing in his barn."

"Prince Charming? You're having me on." Dierdre's gaze bounced uncertainly between Harriet and Reggie.

Reggie blinked, perhaps not familiar with his abductee's name and maybe thinking she was talking about him.

Although *charming* would be the last word Harriet would use to describe him at this moment. "No, I know the Danbys' Suffolk ram."

Reggie jabbed the pitchfork toward her as the sound of the car engine faded.

Not Van after all. To be fair, it was all but impossible for him to make the journey from town so quickly, but she'd still gotten her hopes up. And who could blame her while she was facing the business end of a pitchfork?

Dierdre snorted. "Why would Prince Charming be here? Maybe that's just a ram who resembles him." Then, apparently tracking Harriet's gaze to the pitchfork, Dierdre planted her hands on her hips. "Reggie, what on earth are you doing? Put that down."

"I'm doing it for us, Dierdre." Reggie's tone pleaded with her, though his gaze never left Harriet. "She wants to ruin everything."

"I don't understand."

Harriet prepared to fling herself to the side if Reggie lunged. "Stay back, Dierdre. He's been using you. He's the sheep rustler."

Dierdre laughed. "Don't be ridiculous. Reggie wouldn't do something like that."

Reggie's gaze hardened. Not that Dierdre could see, because he clearly didn't intend to shift his attention off Harriet.

"Reggie?" Dierdre's voice shook. "Tell her she's got it wrong. Tell her it wasn't you."

"Go back to the house," he replied. "I'll be there in a minute."

"Are you trying to cover for my brother? Because I already know he must've helped Zee. You don't have to try to protect me."

"It wasn't Zee or your brother," Harriet said. "It was all Reggie."

Dierdre's face paled. "I don't understand."

"He's been trying to replicate Samuel Bishop's super breed," Harriet said.

"Shut up." Reggie punctuated the order with another threatening jab.

Dierdre latched on to his arm. "Reggie, stop."

Reggie shook her off as if she were a sack of grain. "She'll ruin everything. My new breed will make Springfield Farms great again." Reggie spared her a derisive glance. "She's standing in our way. No one else suspects me."

Dierdre shook her head. "I can't let you do this."

Wrong answer. Harriet squirmed at the visible anger oozing from Reggie's every pore.

He positioned himself so both Harriet and Dierdre were cornered between the empty horse stalls and the barn wall.

Harriet made a break toward the opposite side of the aisle, but Reggie was quicker. He drove the handle of the pitchfork into her stomach.

Dierdre screamed.

Harriet doubled over, gasping from the pain even as she was glad that he hadn't used the sharp end.

"Shut up," Reggie snapped at Dierdre. "I guess you'll have to meet the same end she's heading for."

"Think about it," Dierdre reasoned, her voice trembling. "Even if you manage to create amazing lambs, the minute you try to market them, someone is going to realize that your paperwork doesn't line up."

Reggie smirked at her. "I studied computer science at university, remember? Hacking into government records and adjusting them for my benefit was the easiest part of the whole plan."

Harriet grunted. So Polly's conspiracy-computer-hacker theory was right. She'd have to let her friend know.

If she ever saw Polly again.

Reggie grabbed Dierdre's arm and shoved her toward Harriet. "Move."

"I'm sorry," Dierdre whispered as they shuffled ahead of the pitchfork. "I had no idea what he was doing."

"It's going to be okay," Harriet murmured. "We just need to keep him talking a while longer." A challenge Dierdre was born to meet if ever there was one. "I've already texted Van. As soon as we're close to the door, make a run for it. He can't chase us both if we go in different directions."

"Quiet," Reggie ordered. He directed them away from the barn's main door and toward a smaller one Harriet hadn't noticed before. "In there." When they didn't move, he poked Harriet's back with the pitchfork. "Open the door."

Harriet let out a yelp and quickly obeyed.

The door opened into a small, dusty storage room with no windows.

"The two of you can sit in here until I decide what to do with you." He shoved them in then slammed the door shut.

Harriet grabbed her phone, but before she could unlock her screen, the door burst open once more.

"Toss your phones over here."

Harriet defiantly clung to hers, but he snatched it from her grip.

Before he could do the same to Dierdre, she obediently tossed hers then curled her hands into her chest.

Reggie crushed the phones with his boot. "I'll have your keys too." He held out a hand.

Harriet tossed them to the opposite corner. The instant he bent to retrieve them, she lunged for the door.

But Reggie was faster. He spun around and prodded her back with the pitchfork.

An instant later, the door slammed shut, and the click of a padlock sealed their nightmare.

The room fell into darkness, the silence broken only by Dierdre's sobs.

"We're going to get out of here," Harriet said, even as she fought the impulse to join her. She coughed at the dust they'd stirred. The room smelled intensely of moldy hay and dirt.

She circled the room, unable to see a thing, and lightly ran her fingers along the walls—three wooden and one stone. By the time she'd traversed the perimeter, stepping over Dierdre's huddled form in the process, her eyes had adjusted to the darkness and she could see tiny holes in the wooden walls, each allowing a smidgen of light to sneak in.

"'I am the light of the world. Whoever follows Me will never walk in darkness,'" Harriet recited aloud, for her own comfort as much as Dierdre's. "Please Lord, bring help. Show us the way out."

"I can't believe I didn't see what he was," Dierdre sobbed. "I loved him."

"I know you did," Harriet soothed.

"I've been such a fool."

"He had us all fooled. But right now, we need to come up with a plan. In his mind, we're the one thing standing between him and success. We have to be ready for him because unless he comes to his senses, he's going to try to get rid of us."

"We should've told him the police already know about him."

"At the time, I was afraid that telling him might send him over the edge. Now I'm not so sure staying quiet was the right decision. It might have stopped this." Harriet began to work her way around the room once more. "We need to find something we can use as a weapon. Do you know if he has a gun?"

"I imagine so. My dad has a shotgun to deal with predators. I think most farmers out here do."

Harriet stifled a groan. "That's what I was afraid of."

A noisy engine roared to life.

"That sounds like a tractor," Dierdre said. "What's he doing?"

The noise grew louder.

"It sounds as if he's parked it right outside the barn wall," Harriet said. "He must be hoping the sound will make it impossible for anyone to hear us shouting. If he hides my truck too, anyone who drives in will assume I've left."

"But the police will search the barns, won't they?" Dierdre's voice rose in a frenzied panic. "They have to search the barns."

Harriet was pretty sure that the police had no more right to search the premises without a search warrant in the UK than they did in the US, unless they had reason to believe someone's life was in immediate danger. Would the photo she'd sent of Prince Charming be enough?

Dierdre pressed the back of her fingers to her nose. "Whew, the fumes are going to stink us out."

Harriet clapped both hands over her mouth as she realized the true reason for the tractor's proximity. Reggie had decided to take another page from Samuel Bishop's story and make *them* disappear without a trace too.

Kingsbury Estate, Whitby, and Scarborough
March 24, 1947

Samuel tightened his scarf over his nose and mouth against the biting east wind as he trudged across the heath. His loyal dog matched his steps, his head low, his eyes mere slits.

"Sorry, Shep. I'll make up a warm straw bed for you in Jim's barn before I go." Samuel hadn't wanted to walk the distance from the estate to Whitby alone, but he hadn't expected the trip to be so rough on the dog either. At least the snow still covering the moors was mere inches deep now, rather than feet. "I'd take you with me on the train to Scarborough if I could. But my mate lives in a small flat. You'd hate it there. I shan't be gone more than a fortnight though. I'll be back to fetch you straight after Easter."

Anyone overhearing his one-sided conversation might think he was daft, but even if Shep couldn't understand what he said, the sheepdog seemed to find his voice comforting.

Samuel supposed he should have left word at the estate that he was taking a holiday, but he couldn't bear the thought of more questions about the goings-on at his farm. When Tupper had come to collect his flock and told him to keep the whole business a secret, it had been a grievous time for both him and Shep.

When Gordon's letter arrived, inviting him to visit, it had felt like a godsend. With the sheep gone and little to do until he could restock, there'd never be a more opportune time to visit an old friend he hadn't seen since Gordon's family moved before the war.

Four hours after setting out, Samuel reached Jim's farm. He didn't know the man personally, but Gordon had assured him the fellow farmer wouldn't mind keeping Shep while Samuel was gone. The dog would probably have been happier staying with a neighbor on the estate, but then Samuel would have had to offer an explanation for the trip, which the mischief-makers would no doubt twist into another grand conspiracy.

After getting Shep settled with Jim, Samuel trekked the last miles to the train station.

The train would make several stops along the scenic route, so Samuel settled in for a long ride, grateful to be off his feet and out of the cold. He fell asleep almost before the train left the station and didn't wake until the conductor nudged him at the end of the line.

Gordon's flaming-red hair was visible above all the others on the platform. They embraced, and for the first time since losing his beloved sheep, Samuel began to feel a sense of comfort.

Gordon slapped him on the back. "Good to see you, old chap."

They wound their way through the streets to Gordon's flat. Along the way, Gordon pointed out the reconstruction that had taken place since the war ended. "By the end of next month, they should have most of the repairs made, though I'm not sure they'll ever replace the wrought iron fences they tore out of the parks when they were desperate for more metal."

Samuel shook his head, appreciating once more how far removed he'd been from the effects of the war. While Samuel had been working the farm, Gordon had been called up to fight for king and country. Though farmers were exempted from the conscription, Samuel had volunteered to fight but been rejected when the army doctor found that he had a heart murmur. He'd gone back to his farm and resumed his work. Losing his flock was worse than anything he had faced during the war years, no matter how much he'd been paid for it.

"Last month, they started demolishing the brick surface shelters." Gordon indicated an air-raid shelter in someone's garden. "My landlady says she's keeping hers." He chuckled. "Uses it for her hens."

They enjoyed a simple evening meal together and reminisced well into the night. The next few days passed in similar fashion, with Samuel exploring the town in the mornings while Gordon put in a half day at his work building coaches.

Friday morning, Gordon was surprised when Samuel wasn't up with the sun as usual. He was about to leave for work when an inner compulsion nudged him to check on his old friend.

To his shock, Samuel had passed away in his sleep, likely of the underlying condition that had produced his heart murmur. Since he had no living relatives, Gordon arranged for a private burial in Scarborough. He wrote a letter to Jim in Whitby, asking if he'd keep Shep.

The following week, a condolence letter arrived from Jim. At the end of his note he'd written, I'm afraid Samuel's dog took it into his head to run off, probably to search for his master. We haven't been able to find him.

Was Shep the only one mourning Samuel Bishop? The idea wrenched at Gordon's heart. He made the trip to Samuel's home, intending to settle Samuel's final affairs and perhaps return Shep to Jim's care.

He only succeeded at the former goal. Samuel's faithful sheepdog eluded capture, and Gordon was forced to return home and pick up his own life. But he never forgot about the dog and his unwavering loyalty.

CHAPTER TWENTY-FOUR

Fumes filled the small room, burning Harriet's throat. Beside her, Dierdre coughed. Harriet frantically searched in the dark for the source and finally found the end of a small hose that Reggie must have wedged through a hole near the floor in the stone wall. "Quick," she said to Dierdre. "Hand me your scarf." She stuffed it into the hose and said, "Bang something against the wood wall to knock holes into it for ventilation."

Coughing again, Dierdre kicked at the wall. "It's too thick."

"We have to try." Harriet tried prying rocks from the mortar.

"You'll never get through that either," Dierdre said. "This is impossible."

"We just have to remove enough rocks to chip more holes in the mortar." A heavy chunk of limestone broke free. Testing the weight in her hands, Harriet turned to the door. "I bet that door isn't as thick as the walls." She heaved the rock to her shoulder and hurled it at the door.

It bounced off and fell to the ground.

"I heard it splinter." Dierdre picked up the rock and handed it to Harriet. "Try again."

Harriet wanted to catch her breath, but that was rapidly becoming impossible. Desperation fueled her next throw.

A loud crack split the air.

"It's working." Dierdre handed Harriet the rock again.

Harriet heaved the rock toward the door once more. This time, the rock sailed through the wood, leaving a head-size hole in its wake.

"You did it!" Dierdre cheered.

Harriet shushed Dierdre before her shouts could alert Reggie. "We're not out yet." She reached through the hole and felt around for the door latch. But as she feared, he'd padlocked it. "Get me a smaller rock that I can use like a hammer. Maybe I can break the padlock."

Dierdre rushed to the stone wall and after several moments of grunting, brought Harriet a fist-sized rock. "Will this do?"

"Let's hope so." Harriet reached through the hole. Standing on her tiptoes and bracing her other hand on the wall, she hammered blindly away at the padlock. Sweat slicked her brow. Her muscles burned, and her fingers grew raw from scraping against the rock and wood.

"Let me have a go," Dierdre volunteered.

Harriet drew her hand from the hole then put her nose to it and drew a lungful of the less-toxic air before turning around and handing the rock to Dierdre.

After a few minutes of Dierdre hammering, Harriet thought she heard another engine. "Wait. I hear something."

Dierdre withdrew her hand and put her ear to the opening, covering the other to deaden the competing racket of the tractor. "I think I heard a car door slam. Should we try shouting?"

"Let me have a listen. It could be Reggie moving the Land Rover to hide it." Harriet tried looking through the hole at an angle but could only see the wall on the other side of the barn. "I hear voices," she said. "Male voices." Harriet's chest constricted, her breath stalling in her chest. "That sounds like Zee."

"We should shout," Dierdre said.

"Wait. If Zee's in cahoots with Reggie, he might be here to help him make sure we don't talk. Maybe they'll stage a car accident or something after we've passed out from the carbon monoxide." Harriet pressed her fingers to her forehead, already starting to feel dizzy despite the air hole they'd smashed open.

Barking suddenly erupted.

Dierdre crowded next to Harriet at the opening. "That sounds like Bouncer."

"I know my sister's here!" Tristan shouted, accompanied by frantic barking. "Dierdre?"

Dierdre pounded on the door. "Tristan, we're in here!"

Tristan continued ranting, the sound fading as he apparently searched buildings farther away.

Harriet joined Dierdre in pounding the door. "No, this way! We're in the horse barn!"

The dog must have heard them, because his barking grew louder. Seconds later, he appeared outside the door.

"Good boy, Bouncer," Dierdre praised. "Show Tris. Get Tris."

The dog raced off.

A shotgun blast shook the rafters.

"No," Harriet and Dierdre screamed in unison.

The silence dragged on for what felt like an eternity but was probably less than a minute. A moment later, the barn door creaked and light seeped into the passageway outside their prison. Feet shuffled.

"You won't get away with this," Tristan warned. "The police know you're their rustler. Dr. Bailey texted pictures to them. Pastor Will knows too. He texted me that Dierdre and Doc Bailey were here."

"And we told His Lordship that we were coming here," Zee chimed in.

Harriet's heart swelled. Will had called in the cavalry and was no doubt on his way too.

"Tristan," Dierdre cried when her brother came into view.

He lunged toward the door. "Are you okay?" He had a fat lip and swollen eye.

"Did he shoot…?" Dierdre's voice wobbled as she glanced past the guys.

Harriet's heart squeezed at the realization that the dog was no longer barking and nowhere to be seen.

"That was a warning shot. The next one won't be." Aiming his shotgun at Tristan and Zee, Reggie sneered at the state of his supply room door. "Been busy, I see." He tossed a key to Zee. "Open it."

When Zee stationed his hulking figure in front of the padlock, he completely blocked Reggie from view. "The second this door is open, run," he said under his breath. "We'll cover you."

Harriet's heart stampeded at the click of the lock.

Zee slowly twisted open the padlock and unhooked it from the mangled lock's eyes.

"Now get in there with them," Reggie ordered.

"Get ready," Zee whispered, reaching for the door handle as Tristan stepped clear of the direction the door would swing. The pair of them effectively formed a barricade between the women and Reggie's shotgun. "Now!"

Tristan let out a piercing whistle, and Bouncer, who must have been quietly awaiting his master's next command, exploded onto the scene and took a flying leap at Reggie's arm.

Harriet and Dierdre ran from the barn.

The sudden light was blinding.

Strong arms swallowed her, and Harriet flailed. "Let go of me!"

"Harriet, it's me. It's Will." His words broke through the fog of terror. "You're safe."

"Will?" She melted against him. "Thank goodness."

"Tristan and Zee are still in there," Dierdre said. "And Reggie has a shotgun."

Will hurried Harriet away from the barns as Van steered Dierdre clear and radioed for armed backup.

"Are you okay?" Will pulled back to search her eyes.

"He locked us in a supply closet and piped tractor exhaust inside to try to suffocate us."

"Do you feel dizzy?" He cupped her face in his hands. "Nauseous? Weak? Headache? Any chest pain?"

"My pulse is going crazy, but I think that's the adrenaline. I managed to stuff the pipe to slow the exhaust, and we knocked a hole in the door." The ground suddenly seemed to shift beneath her feet. "Maybe I am a little dizzy."

"We'll need to get you and Dierdre examined by medical professionals."

"Reggie Springfield," Van bellowed. "This is the police. Drop your weapon and come out with your hands up."

Bouncer raced from the barn, yipping happily.

A moment later, Tristan and Zee appeared with a trussed-up Reggie hoisted between them. Zee now sported a bloody nose and swollen eye too, confirming that Reggie hadn't given up without a fight.

The instant Van relieved the guys of their charge, Dierdre threw her arms around her brother. Then she drew back and swatted his arm. "What were you thinking? You could have been killed."

"I was thinking I had to keep my baby sister safe, but I don't need thanks for that." Tristan chuckled. "You should thank the pastor. He's the one who begged us to get over here and watch out for you until the police arrived."

Harriet squeezed Will's hand and laid her head on his shoulder. "My hero."

"When I spotted Doc Bailey's vehicle in the implement shed, I knew you had to be here somewhere," Tristan explained.

Harriet strode over to Zee and extended her hand. "I owe you an apology."

Zee shook her hand. "Don't worry about it. This isn't the first time my nose has been broken."

Harriet ducked her head. "For that too. But mostly for suspecting you might be involved in the sheep rustling."

He gaped at her and then burst into laughter. "You thought I was stealing sheep?"

Harriet squirmed. "I'm ashamed to say I did. I misjudged you simply because you look a little scary…"

"And you act like a grouch." Tristan elbowed his friend. "Didn't I tell you? Everyone misreads you. You've got to work on that." To

Harriet, Tristan said, "He's a super nice guy when you get to know him. But he's so shy that people assume he doesn't want anything to do with them or has something to hide."

Zee frowned. "Tristan's trying to help, but I'm afraid I'm a lost cause."

"No one's a lost cause," Tristan corrected him. "Except maybe Reggie there. We'll get you sorted out." He grinned at his sister. "I never liked that guy, you know."

Dierdre rolled her eyes. "Don't worry. I don't think it's going to work out with him."

"I was wrong to jump to conclusions," Harriet told Zee. "I'm sincerely sorry."

Zee's cheeks reddened as he waved her words away. "Apology accepted."

"Now that smile makes you seem not nearly so scary," Harriet teased, "even with the swollen eye and broken nose."

Will curled his arm around Harriet's waist and tugged her close once again. "Everyone looks better when they've just saved your life."

Harriet had to agree.

Late Monday afternoon, Will surprised Harriet at Cobble Hill, wearing a kangaroo pouch strapped over his chest with a tiny gray kitten peeking over the edge.

"Look at *you*," Harriet cooed, scratching its fuzzy head. "I love seeing your eyes open. They're beautiful."

"Dierdre can't keep up with feedings now that she's back in school," Will explained. "And her mum didn't have time. So I volunteered to take Ash Wednesday. Ash for short. We really connected when we met the other day."

"I can't think of a better home for him," Harriet said. "What about the other three?"

"Vivien's grandson volunteered to help Vivien care for them until two are ready to be adopted out. I think she knows which one she's keeping already." Will rubbed Ash's cheek, beaming when the kitten produced a small purr. "I didn't want Ash to get lonely without his sisters, so I figured I'd carry him around this way. Keeps him warm and helps to socialize him as well. He'll need good social skills as a church cat."

Harriet grinned at the adorable pair. "It's a wonderful idea. You'll have a friend for life."

"That's not all I came to tell you. Van says they've finished processing the evidence at the Springfield Farm, and he's invited the farmers whose sheep were stolen to go there to get them back."

"How wonderful."

"And since you were instrumental in solving the case, he's invited us to go." Will's eyes beamed with pride. "He thought the farmers might also appreciate your medical opinion on the condition of their stock."

"Absolutely. I'd be happy to come." Throwing caution to the wind that she wouldn't get an emergency call, Harriet also agreed to ride with Will rather than drive herself.

"How's Dierdre doing?" Harriet asked as they drove to the farm. "I assume you talked to her when you picked up Ash. I've been so preoccupied with writing my article that I'm afraid I haven't talked to her since everything happened."

"Currently, she's too angry at Reggie to be sad about losing him. But I'm afraid she feels guilty about her unwitting role in the thefts. I spoke to Doreen, and she said she would call to reassure Dierdre that none of the farmers blame her in the least."

"Doreen's a gem. I would hate to see this set Dierdre back. Her enthusiasm for a veterinary career is truly inspiring."

"How's your article coming along?"

"I hope to finish it tonight," Harriet said. "I would have finished it by now, but I got distracted with research. I spent all of yesterday afternoon at the estate, finishing going through Samuel Bishop's journals."

"I don't suppose you managed to figure out what happened to him," Will said.

"Actually, I did. If anyone had read his last journal all the way through, they would have learned about it at the end. He writes about going out of town to visit an old friend. His super-breed actually survived the blizzard, which made it a raging success. But the government still pulled the plug on it, saying they didn't realize it would take multiple generations to finish the experiment and that it was too expensive. They confiscated his entire flock and swore him to secrecy, though they paid him for the work he'd already done."

"So did he quit farming?" Will asked.

"I don't think so. I believe he meant to take a well-earned vacation then return to rebuild his flock. The last entry in his journal is a note from the friend he went to visit. Gordon explains that Samuel passed away in his sleep from an untreated heart condition during his visit."

Will's face fell. "That's terrible. But why has no one discovered this before?"

"Samuel had no living relatives. Gordon must have figured that if anyone else was curious about it, they'd consult Samuel's journals, which Gordon gave to the estate for their records. My guess is that none of his contemporaries knew about the journals or had the time to investigate. Idle chatter probably produced the ghost story legend and the Russian assassin rumor, both of which were much more fun to spread than finding out the facts anyway. The truth was right there all along for anyone who bothered to look."

"Wow. Will you tell Samuel's story?"

"I don't think so. Something tells me the town's ghost-story enthusiasts wouldn't thank me for it."

"Too right." Will tossed her a wink. "Will you use the mysterious version for your article's opening hook?"

"Actually, I wrote two potential openings. Aunt Jinny and Polly both think Tristan's story makes a stronger hook."

"Tristan's story?"

Harriet's grin widened. "His new side business teaching kids how to train their dogs to herd sheep. I don't know how many of them will actually use the training when they're older, but either way, it's a productive use of their time, and it's a good hobby to have."

"Okay, then. Polly and Jinny are right. That is a good hook." Will drove into the farmyard and parked behind Van's cruiser. He got out and came to open the door for Harriet.

An elderly man emerged from the barn as Van joined them.

"Is that Reggie's grandfather?" Harriet asked.

"Aye," Van confirmed. "Reggie claims his grandfather knew nothing and wasn't involved in any way. Not sure I believe him, but at least this way someone's here to take care of the livestock until Reggie makes bail."

"Have you found out why he did all this?" Will asked Van.

"He's made a full confession. Like so many other small farms, his grandfather's farm has been struggling financially for a while now. Having grown up in the area, Reggie's heard the legend of Samuel Bishop for years, and he decided to try to recreate Bishop's super-breed to end the farm's financial troubles. He didn't have the capital to acquire the animals legally, so he decided to minimize cost and maximize profit."

"By stealing them," Harriet filled in. "I can't imagine how he thought he'd get away with that in a tight-knit community like this one."

"He was planning to breed them out of the usual season then return the animals he took after he had gotten their contributions to his super-breed. In his mind, it was foolproof," Van explained.

"Did Reggie reveal how he accessed the Danbys' pasture?" Harriet asked.

Van nodded. "From your place, as you suspected. Dierdre had mentioned you would be out for the evening."

Harriet shuddered. "So the next time Maxwell barks at an engine noise, I should investigate more closely."

"But not alone," Will told her. "Call me first."

Her heart warmed at the concern in his voice. "Deal."

Van led them to the barn where the stolen sheep had been relocated. "If you could check them over first, I'll bring the farmers in as they arrive."

"No problem." There were several more than the ones Harriet had found Saturday. She examined each animal thoroughly and was glad to find them no worse for wear. It made sense, since Reggie had planned to use them to create a new super-breed, that he would want them in peak condition.

By the time Van returned with the farmers whose sheep had been stolen, Harriet had finished her examinations and declared them all healthy.

The farmers reclaimed their livestock, many with tears of joy glistening in their eyes. As Doreen led the parade of sheep out of the barn, each farmer stopped and shook Harriet's hand with exuberant gratitude. A few even hugged her. All informed her they would bring future veterinary needs to her.

Mr. Digger approached her last. "I'm right grateful to you, lass. We're privileged to have you here, and if anyone tells you differently, you send them to me. I'll set them straight."

Harriet smiled at his earnest promise. "Thank you. I appreciate your confidence in me."

Doreen had drawn Prince Charming off to the side and was waiting to speak to Harriet. "Didn't I tell you?"

Her heart bursting with joy, Harriet laughed. "Yes, you did."

Grinning, Will pressed a kiss to her temple.

Doreen's eyes widened. "You two are a couple?"

"We are indeed," Will proclaimed, the pride in his voice making Harriet's heart skip a beat.

"How did I not know this?" Doreen demanded.

"We were keeping it under wraps so we could see how it went without pressure," Harriet explained.

Will wrapped his arm around her. "But I'm too happy to hide it anymore."

"Me too," Harriet told him.

As he lowered his head to kiss her, Harriet reflected that whether it was missing sheep or hidden relationships, the truth would always come to light in White Church Bay.

FROM THE AUTHOR

Dear Reader,

When I was invited to pen a second Cobble Hill Farm mystery, this one set in February, I immediately researched three things—the weather in Yorkshire at that time of year, special events, and what's happening on the farms. Discovering that lambing begins, that the school's half-term break coincides with the Dark Nights Festival, and of course Valentine's Day, I knew I wanted to include them all. Yet I soon found my research snowballing. It began with researching sheep rustling, which turned out to be a far more widespread and difficult-to-prosecute offense than I anticipated.

Researching the history of sheep breeds opened up an entirely new dimension to the story. But it was in subscribing to the UK's *Farmers Weekly* and reading the articles each week that I came to truly appreciate how increasingly challenging it is for farmers, especially those on small holdings, to survive, let alone thrive, and inspired the motivation for my culprit.

The idyllic setting of the sheep-farming community and the hardworking men and women who carry on the family farms from generation to generation formed an intriguing backdrop to explore what Harriet needed to learn about herself to solve the mystery of the disappearing sheep.

Harriet, like many of us, is quick to judge those who *look* like bad guys, either because of their checkered past, their appearance or demeanor, or even their friends. Yet she discovers that negative appearances can be equally deceiving.

Have you ever wondered how many connections with remarkable individuals have been missed because preconceived judgments based on appearances, speech, profession, or hearsay caused you to overlook their potential? As I delved into Harriet's narrative, I felt encouraged to adopt a more discerning approach in every encounter. I hope you do too.

Signed,
Sandra Orchard

ABOUT THE AUTHOR

Sandra Orchard writes fast-paced, keep-you-guessing stories with a generous dash of sweet romance. Touted by Midwest Book Reviews as "a true master of the [mystery] genre," Sandra is also a best-selling romantic suspense author. Her novels have garnered numerous Canadian Christian writing awards, as well as an RT Reviewers' Choice Award, a National Readers' Choice Award, a Holt Medallion, and a Daphne du Maurier Award of Excellence. When not plotting fictional crimes, Sandra enjoys hiking with her hubby, working in their vegetable gardens, and playing make-believe with their dozen-plus young grandchildren. Sandra hails from Niagara, Canada, and loves to hear from readers.

A STROLL THROUGH THE ENGLISH COUNTRYSIDE

The International Dark Sky Reserve designated North York Moors National Park—a real place near our fictional town of White Church Bay—a Dark Sky Reserve in December 2020. At the time, it and six other UK locations were among only twenty-one such places in the world. But as more countries have recognized the value of preserving our night skies, that number has grown to more than 200 worldwide.

Dark nights are important for the proper functioning of many human and animal biological systems, as well as for proper plant growth. The goal of Dark Sky locations is to preserve the night sky by reducing or eliminating artificial outdoor lighting, as well as to educate and elevate awareness of the importance of doing so.

For residents and visitors alike, the vast dark skies over North York Moors National Park furnish spectacular stargazing opportunities. Where the skies are the darkest, as many as 2000 stars, as well as planets and their moons can be seen at one time. Twice a year, the park hosts special festivals—the Dark Skies Festival for two weeks in February and the Dark Skies Fringe Festival during the school's half-term break in October. During the festivals, local businesses and organizations offer unique opportunities to enjoy and/or learn more about the night sky, although such opportunities also abound throughout the year.

Take a moonlit walk while exploring nocturnal nature to spot owls, bats, and other creatures. Enjoy a campfire dinner or sleep under the stars. Learn how to navigate at night. Stargaze or take the experience one step further by participating in astronomer-led opportunities, complete with a variety of telescopes. Take a night-time photography workshop. Or enjoy a coastal walk, a ghost walk, or join your little ones on the children's trails. Then while waiting for nightfall to return, enjoy daytime activities such as bat-box building, watercolor painting, and various other crafts.

Of even greater worth is the immeasurable benefits the awe-inspiring beauty of a vast night sky gives our spirit. Drinking in the magnificence is truly a glorious reminder of the marvelous work of our Lord and Creator. And if you're visiting Yorkshire, enjoying a star-filled night sky in North York Moors National Park is an experience not to be missed.

YORKSHIRE YUMMIES

Yorkshire Pudding

Ingredients:

4 large eggs

1 cup milk

1 pinch salt

1 cup all-purpose flour

2 tablespoons beef drippings, lard or vegetable oil (not oils with a low smoke point)

Directions:

1) Thoroughly whisk eggs, milk, and pinch of salt in a bowl and let stand for 10 minutes.

2) Sift flour into egg and milk mixture. Whisk well so there are no lumps. Let sit in refrigerator at least 30 minutes to allow time to rise and chill.

3) Preheat oven to 425°F. Do not use convection.

4) Spoon ½ teaspoon fat into each section of a 12-hole muffin tin. Ideally use a tin that's only been wiped clean between batches, not washed with soap and water, which can cause puddings to stick and not rise properly. Heat until smoking—about 5 minutes.

5) Quickly fill muffin cups ⅓ to ½ full and immediately return to oven.

6) Bake 20 to 25 minutes until puffed up and golden brown. Resist the temptation to open the door before they are finished baking, or pudding will likely sink.
7) Serve immediately. Can be refrigerated in an airtight container for 3 days and reheated at 350°F for 10 minutes.

Tips: Make sure batter is cold and completely smooth, and oven is hot before cooking. Do not open the oven door during cooking. Keep baked puddings away from drafts.

Snake in the Grass

BY ELIZABETH PENNEY

Spring had finally come to Cobble Hill Farm, in White Church Bay, Yorkshire. Yellow daffodils nodded in cheerful bunches, lambs gamboled in the fields, and the sun's warmth was making a welcome return. New life unfurled in every direction, and as a result, Dr. Harriet Bailey had a bad case of spring fever.

Not that she wasn't busy. The vet practice had been slammed all day, on top of a busy week. "Goodbye," Harriet called to the last patient, a woman with two cockapoos needing annual checkups. "Thanks for coming in." As soon as the door closed behind them, she faced Polly Thatcher, her twenty-five-year-old assistant. "Ready for a break? I'm wiped."

Polly tapped a few more keys then pushed back from her desk, blond ponytail swinging. "I sure am. Let's have tea and a snack, and then I'll finish the files."

Noticing the circles under her assistant's eyes, Harriet made an executive decision. "No you won't. It's Friday afternoon, and you're going home to put your feet up." Anticipating Polly's protest, she lifted a hand. "For once, Saturday appointments are sparse, so the paperwork can wait until Monday." The weather was supposed to be good this weekend, the first really warm March days, and people had plans.

Polly grinned as she rolled her chair forward. "I'll log out before you change your mind."

"And I'll go put the kettle on."

She went through the door into the main house. Last year, at age thirty-three, Harriet had moved from Connecticut to England to take over the veterinary practice owned by her late grandfather, Harold Bailey, and his father before him. She'd had big shoes to fill, and there had been some challenges, but Harriet now felt firmly established and at home in White Church Bay.

Harriet's lone regret was that she hadn't come to England sooner and worked with her grandfather before he died. According to her aunt, Dr. Jinny Garrett—a physician who lived in the dower cottage on the property—he had been very proud of Harriet and her achievements in the field. Harriet had been busy working in a large practice Stateside and planning to marry a fellow veterinarian.

Then that relationship had fallen apart, and her beloved grandfather had passed away, leaving his home and his practice to her. Her whole world had been turned upside down.

"Things have a way of working out for the best," Harriet murmured as she filled the kettle. She was dating Pastor Will Knight, a kind man and a good friend, on a casual basis. It was too soon to think about the future. She was having too much fun enjoying the present.

Wondering if she should have coffee instead, Harriet eyed the single-serve coffee machine, one of the few modern touches in the kitchen. The two-hundred-year-old stone farmhouse had never been fully renovated. Harriet appreciated the flagstone and wood floors, the plaster walls, and the beamed ceilings. It wasn't just a house, it was a piece of history—North Yorkshire's and her own.

She chose a French roast pod and started the coffeemaker. According to the temperature on the window thermometer, it was hovering in the fifties. Harriet decided they should sit outside in the sun for the first time since December, even though Yorkshire winters weren't quite as cold as Connecticut's. She hadn't missed the heaps of snow one bit. Her parents were a different story. She missed them every day. Hopefully, they would visit again soon, as they had for Thanksgiving.

Charlie, the clinic's calico cat, bolted into the room. The clinic's dachshund, Maxwell, was right behind her, the wheels that supported his paralyzed hindquarters spinning madly. Harriet laughed. "You two must have spring fever too." Their response was to hurry to her feet, where they looked up at her with hopeful eyes. "I'll give you snacks outside. How's that?"

The pets dashed to the French doors to wait, drawing another laugh from Harriet.

"What's going on?" Polly asked as she came through from the clinic.

"These guys." In the middle of preparing a tray, Harriet pointed with her chin. "I thought we could sit outside." Along with the pet treats, she added the latest goodies from her neighbor Doreen Danby, a great baker. "Doreen brought over raspberry-filled sugar cookies today."

"Oh, yum." Polly peered into the tin. "Love those." The kettle whistled, and she added a teabag to a mug then filled it with boiling water.

Polly held the door for Harriet, who carried the tray, and the foursome paraded onto the back patio. Harriet narrowly avoided tripping over the eager dog and cat.

Harriet dispensed the pet treats before joining Polly at the table. The low afternoon sun still gave off heat, and she lifted her face to savor it. Her heart expanded with each breath of air tinged with the scent of green, growing things.

Then an all-too-familiar feeling of restlessness churned, and she squirmed in the chair, trying to get comfortable.

"What's up?" Polly asked. She didn't miss a trick—or any nuance indicating Harriet's state of mind. "You're frowning."

"I am?" Harriet rubbed her fingers across her forehead, hoping she wasn't developing lines. "I feel like a racehorse waiting for the gun to fire. I'm champing at the bit."

Polly nodded. "It's time for some new adventures. Winter can be a long, hard slog, one foot in front of the other, just trying to get through."

"You're absolutely right. Not to mention the dubious fun of dealing with snow and ice and bitter cold on farm visits." Harriet rolled her eyes. While many trips had thankfully involved seeing animals in warm barns and shelters, she'd been out in the fields quite often.

She returned to Polly's first point. "When you said new adventures, did you have anything in mind?"

Polly leaned across the table, eagerness shining on her pretty face. "You know Captain Ezra?"

"He has a Newfoundland named Ursula. Yes." Harriet often remembered clinic clients by their pets.

"That's right. As you know, Captain Ezra does boat tours in the summer out of Whitby Harbor. He offered to take us out on Sunday if we wanted. He likes to perform a few trial runs to make sure everything is working right before the season starts."

"Us?" Harriet inquired. "Who else is going?"

Polly shrugged. "I'm not sure. 'Bring a friend—or two,' he said. That's why I asked you."

But not Detective Constable Van Worthington. Polly and Van had started dating last fall, only to have a rather dramatic breakup when Van proposed before Polly was ready. Harriet had seen indications that Polly was revisiting her decision, but the two were still wary around each other.

Harriet pulled out her phone. "I'll see if Will wants to go." As she typed the text, she asked, "Any other ideas?"

"Maybe." Polly snagged another cookie. "I'll give it some thought." After swallowing a bite, she said, "There should be some professional seminars, conferences, and workshops coming up too. Doc Bailey used to attend them now and again. He said they kept him sharp."

"That's a good point." Harriet thought back over the previous year as she sent the text. "With the move and settling in, I haven't been to anything like that here."

A car door slammed in the parking lot. "I wonder who that is," Polly said. "Your aunt's office is closed, right?" Like Harriet, Aunt Jinny's practice was attached to her home.

"I believe so. Maybe it's a visitor." Hopefully it wasn't an emergency for either of them, although people generally called first.

Two high, piping voices rang out, and a moment later, a boy and girl appeared around the corner, dressed in matching wool jumpers and jeans. "Harriet!" they cried. Sophie and Sebastian Garrett were Aunt Jinny's twin grandchildren.

The pair engulfed Harriet in hugs. "What are you doing here?" she asked.

"We came for the weekend," Sebastian said. "We all got out early today."

"Do your parents know you're over here?" Harriet asked. "And say hello to Polly."

"Hello, Polly," they chorused obediently.

"We told them we were going to play out here," Sophie added to Harriet.

Next door, Aunt Jinny emerged from her house and waved, letting Harriet know she was aware of the twins' location. "Stay right here." She watched Aunt Jinny settle at her backyard table, obviously planning to keep an eye on them.

"We will," Sebastian promised. Then he noticed the tin of cookies. "Can we have one?"

In response, Harriet held up the tin so Aunt Jinny could see it and then pointed at the youngsters. Aunt Jinny put up one finger.

"Just one," Harriet said. The pair took their time studying the choices, then each took a cookie and ran off.

"They are so cute," Polly said.

Harriet's phone beeped. "Will would like to go. What time should I tell him?" As the local minister, he was tied up with church duties all morning on Sundays.

"One o'clock in Whitby," Polly said. "We can bring a picnic lunch on the boat."

Whitby wasn't too far. "So come back here after church and change, grab our lunch, and go?" Harriet mused. "It's a plan."

The twins poked around the stone wall, followed closely by Charlie and Maxwell. Harriet smiled, thinking about the days she'd been content to play outside with nothing but her imagination.

Next door, Aunt Jinny's son, Anthony, and his wife, Olivia, emerged from the house, tea mugs in hand. As they settled at the table, Harriet said, "Let's go say hi." She grabbed her mug and the tin of cookies.

Polly readily followed, having already formed friendships with the couple, who were about Harriet's age. The family lived in nearby Pickering, and Anthony was a pharmacist while Olivia worked as a kindergarten teacher.

Olivia jumped up as the women approached, and hugged them. "So good to see you. We're here for a relaxing evening." She winked. "I hope."

Anthony had risen to his feet to hug his cousin. "We've both been going at a breakneck pace lately. As for the children, they have a bad case of spring fever."

Sebastian was attempting to shimmy up a large tree trunk while Sophie was walking along the low wall. "Be careful," their mother called. The twins waved but kept on.

"We all do," Harriet said, pulling out a chair. "Cookie—I mean, biscuit?" She offered the tin.

"Don't mind if I do," Anthony said, selecting one. "We're getting fish and chips tonight, and nothing dampens my appetite for that meal."

Olivia laughed. "That one has a hollow leg."

"Tell me about it," Aunt Jinny said. "Couldn't keep him full when he was a boy."

"That sounds good," Harriet said. "Would you mind if I join you?" Cliffside Chippy, a short walk down the public path to the village, was one of Harriet's favorite eateries.

Polly lifted a hand. "Me too, if that's okay. I don't have any dinner plans."

Aunt Jinny regarded her with a sympathetic gaze. She knew all about Polly and Van. "You're both welcome. Any time."

The twins were now kneeling on the ground, studying the stone wall. Sebastian lowered himself even farther, almost lying down, and reached his hand into what looked like a cavity.

Harriet stood up to see better, hoping they hadn't come across an animal that might bite them or a bee's nest.

Sebastian scrambled to his feet, something clutched in both hands, and ran toward the adults, Sophie on his heels.

"Look what I found," he said when he arrived at the table.

Olivia pulled away with a shriek. "That lizard is huge!"

Harriet's heart rate spiked. This was no native reptile. Dull gray, with patches of rusty orange and a small dorsal crest, it looked like an iguana, albeit a species she'd never seen before. Someone's stray pet? With lows still in the thirties, it wasn't safe for this tropical animal to remain loose.

Harriet held out her hands. "Give it to me."

Sebastian readily handed over the creature, whose round dark eyes barely blinked. Its body was a little over a foot long, and it weighed under a pound, if she had to guess.

"Any idea what kind it is?" Anthony asked. "I've never seen one like that before."

"Not off the top of my head." Harriet looked at Polly. "Want to take a picture and do an image search?" While not infallible, an online search would be a start. "We can also post the picture on the local bulletin boards in case someone lost him. Or her." Harriet hadn't treated iguanas or many reptiles before, so she would appreciate help with identification.

Harriet held the iguana in both hands so Polly could get a full-length picture. Fortunately, the lizard didn't pull out of her grip and run. Instead, it seemed quite content to rest.

Everyone waited as Polly searched on her phone. After a couple of minutes, she gasped. "You're not going to believe this." She turned the screen to show them. "It's an endangered rock iguana from the Caribbean. There are only a couple hundred of them left in the world."

A NOTE FROM THE EDITORS

We hope you enjoyed another exciting volume in the Mysteries of Cobble Hill Farm series, published by Guideposts. For over seventy-five years, Guideposts, a nonprofit organization, has been driven by a vision of a world filled with hope. We aspire to be the voice of a trusted friend, a friend who makes you feel more hopeful and connected.

By making a purchase from Guideposts, you join our community in touching millions of lives, inspiring them to believe that all things are possible through faith, hope, and prayer. Your continued support allows us to provide uplifting resources to those in need. Whether through our communities, websites, apps, or publications, we inspire our audiences, bring them together, and comfort, uplift, entertain, and guide them. Visit us at guideposts.org to learn more.

We would love to hear from you. Write us at Guideposts, P.O. Box 5815, Harlan, Iowa 51593 or call us at (800) 932-2145. Did you love *Wolves in Sheep's Clothing*? Leave a review for this product on guideposts.org/shop. Your feedback helps others in our community find relevant products.

Find inspiration, find faith, find Guideposts.

Shop our best sellers and favorites at
guideposts.org/shop

Or scan the QR code to go directly to our Shop

Loved Mysteries of Cobble Hill Farm? Check out some other Guideposts mystery series! Visit https://www.shopguideposts.org/fiction-books/ mystery-fiction.html for more information.

SECRETS FROM GRANDMA'S ATTIC

Life is recorded not only in decades or years, but in events and memories that form the fabric of our being. Follow Tracy Doyle, Amy Allen, and Robin Davisson, the granddaughters of the recently deceased centenarian, Pearl Allen, as they explore the treasures found in the attic of Grandma Pearl's Victorian home, nestled near the banks of the Mississippi in Canton, Missouri. Not only do Pearl's descendants uncover a long-buried mystery at every attic exploration, they also discover their grandmother's legacy of deep, abiding faith, which has shaped and guided their family through the years. These uncovered Secrets from Grandma's Attic reveal stories of faith, redemption, and second chances that capture your heart long after you turn the last page.

History Lost and Found
The Art of Deception
Testament to a Patriot
Buttoned Up

Pearl of Great Price
Hidden Riches
Movers and Shakers
The Eye of the Cat
Refined by Fire
The Prince and the Popper
Something Shady
Duel Threat
A Royal Tea
The Heart of a Hero
Fractured Beauty
A Shadowy Past
In Its Time
Nothing Gold Can Stay
The Cameo Clue
Veiled Intentions
Turn Back the Dial
A Marathon of Kindness
A Thief in the Night
Coming Home

SAVANNAH SECRETS

Welcome to Savannah, Georgia, a picture-perfect Southern city known for its manicured parks, moss-covered oaks, and antebellum architecture. Walk down one of the cobblestone streets, and you'll come upon Magnolia Investigations. It is here where two friends have joined forces to unravel some of Savannah's deepest secrets. Tag along as clues are exposed, red herrings discarded, and thrilling surprises revealed. Find inspiration in the special bond between Meredith Bellefontaine and Julia Foley. Cheer the friends on as they listen to their hearts and rely on their faith to solve each new case that comes their way.

The Hidden Gate
A Fallen Petal
Double Trouble
Whispering Bells
Where Time Stood Still
The Weight of Years
Willful Transgressions
Season's Meetings
Southern Fried Secrets
The Greatest of These
Patterns of Deception

MYSTERIES OF MARTHA'S VINEYARD

Priscilla Latham Grant has inherited a lighthouse! So with not much more than a strong will and a sore heart, the recent widow says goodbye to her lifelong Kansas home and heads to the quaint and historic island of Martha's Vineyard, Massachusetts. There, she comes face-to-face with adventures, which include her trusty canine friend, Jake, three delightful cousins she didn't know she had, and Gerald O'Bannon, a handsome Coast Guard captain—plus head-scratching mysteries that crop up with surprising regularity.

A Light in the Darkness
Like a Fish Out of Water
Adrift
Maiden of the Mist
Making Waves
Don't Rock the Boat
A Port in the Storm
Thicker Than Water
Swept Away
Bridge Over Troubled Waters
Smoke on the Water
Shifting Sands
Shark Bait

Seascape in Shadows
Storm Tide
Water Flows Uphill
Catch of the Day
Beyond the Sea
Wider Than an Ocean
Sheeps Passing in the Night
Sail Away Home
Waves of Doubt
Lifeline
Flotsam & Jetsam
Just Over the Horizon

Find more inspiring stories in these best-loved Guideposts fiction series!

Mysteries of Lancaster County

Follow the Classen sisters as they unravel clues and uncover hidden secrets in Mysteries of Lancaster County. As you get to know these women and their friends, you'll see how God brings each of them together for a fresh start in life.

Secrets of Wayfarers Inn

Retired schoolteachers find themselves owners of an old warehouse-turned-inn that is filled with hidden passages, buried secrets, and stunning surprises that will set them on a course to puzzling mysteries from the Underground Railroad.

Tearoom Mysteries Series

Mix one stately Victorian home, a charming lakeside town in Maine, and two adventurous cousins with a passion for tea and hospitality. Add a large scoop of intriguing mystery, and sprinkle generously with faith, family, and friends, and you have the recipe for *Tearoom Mysteries*.

Ordinary Women of the Bible

Richly imagined stories—based on facts from the Bible—have all the plot twists and suspense of a great mystery, while bringing you fascinating insights on what it was like to be a woman living in the ancient world.

To learn more about these books, visit Guideposts.org/Shop